WHO NEEDS FEMINISM?

WHO NEEDS FEMINISM?

Male Responses to Sexism
in the Church

Edited by
Richard Holloway

First published in Great Britain 1991
SPCK
Holy Trinity Church
Marylebone Road
London NW1 4DU

British Library Cataloguing in Publication Data

Who needs feminism?
  1. Christianity. Women
  I. Holloway, Richard 1933–
262.15

  ISBN 0–281–04543–7

Typeset by Pioneer Associates, Perthshire
Printed in Great Britain by
Biddles Ltd, Guildford and King's Lynn

Contents

The Contributors

RICHARD HOLLOWAY is Bishop of Edinburgh. A well-known writer and broadcaster, his most recent book is *Another Country, Another King* (1991).

STEPHEN C. BARTON is Lecturer in New Testament in the Department of Theology, Durham University. An Australian, he was previously a Tutor in Biblical Studies at Salisbury and Wells Theological College.

L. WILLIAM COUNTRYMAN is Associate Professor of New Testament at the Church Divinity School of the Pacific, Berkeley, California. His most recent books include *Biblical Authority or Biblical Tyranny?* (1981) and *Dirt, Greed and Sex: Sexual Ethics in the New Testament and their Implications for Today* (1988).

MICHAEL JACOBS is an Anglican priest who teaches counselling and psychotherapy at the University of Leicester. Among his recent books are *Swift to Hear* (1985) and *Psycho-dynamic Counselling in Action* (1988).

JOHN KENT is Emeritus Professor of Theology at the University of Bristol. His most recent book is *The Unacceptable Face: The Modern Church and the Historian* (1987).

JAMES P. MACKEY is Thomas Chalmers Professor of Theology at the University of Edinburgh. He has presented programmes on Channel 4 and his most recent books include *A Sense of Direction* (1987) and (with James D. G. Dunn) *New Testament Theology in Dialogue* (1988).

CHRISTOPHER ROWLAND is Dean Ireland's Professor of the Exegesis of Holy Scripture at Oxford. His recent books include *Christian Origins* (1985) and (with Mark Corner) *Liberating Exegesis: The Challenge of Liberation Theology to Biblical Studies* (1990).

PETER SELBY is the Bishop of Kingston. For eight years he was Diocesan Missioner in Newcastle-upon-Tyne. His most recent book is *BeLonging: Challenge to a Tribal Church* (1991).

The Contributors

PHILIP SHELDRAKE SJ is Lecturer in Pastoral Theology and Co-Director of the Institute of Spirituality at Heythrop College, London. He is Co-editor of *The Way* and author of *Images of Holiness* (1987) and *Spirituality and History* (1991).

IAIN TORRANCE is a minister of the Church of Scotland and a Lecturer in Theology at the University of Birmingham. He is Co-editor of the *Scottish Journal of Theology* and author of *Christology after Chalcedon* (1988).

BRIAN WREN is a minister in the United Reformed Church, working freelance as a poet, theologian and worship educator. He is a well-known author and hymn writer. His most recent book is *What Language Shall I Borrow?: A Male Response to Feminist Theology* (1989).

RICHARD HOLLOWAY

Introduction

In a letter written in 1907 Evelyn Underhill said that the keys of
the Catholic position were the incarnation and a mystical
continuation of the incarnation in the sacraments.[1] She was
referring to the most specific of all the Christian doctrines that, in
the person of Jesus Christ, God assumed human nature; in the
words of the Fourth Gospel, the Word became flesh. The doctrine
of the incarnation has profound consequences, sometimes more
honoured in the breach than in the observance, that have infused
Christian history with the pain of discovery and development.
When the apostle Peter had a vision at Joppa of a great sheet let
down from heaven, containing creatures that were held to be
unclean and therefore forbidden to a Jew, he was dismayed to hear
the divine command, bidding him kill and eat. 'No, Lord,' he
replied, 'for nothing common or unclean has ever entered my
mouth.' But the heavenly voice replied, 'What God has cleansed
you must not call common' (Acts 11.5–9). We know from the New
Testament how difficult it was for the first Christians, all of them
Jews like Jesus, to accept the consequences of their belief that
Jesus Christ was the incarnation of God. It affected their attitude
to uncircumcised gentiles, to meat that had been dedicated to idols
in the public market (1 Cor. 8.1–13) and to a whole range of ritual
practices that had to do with a theory of purity that rendered not
only certain foods unclean, but certain people some of the time and
some people all of the time. William Countryman has shown in his
book *Dirt, Greed and Sex*, as well as in his essay in this book, that
what is at issue here is our access to God and obstacles to that
access.

There are two profound implications of the belief that 'God was
in Christ reconciling the world to himself' (2 Cor. 5.19). The first
is that matter has itself become at least potentially sacred, the
vehicle of the divine. The very stuff of creation is revelatory and is
to be celebrated, acknowledged as good, in distinction to any
theories or religions that discount and suspect matter or are
selective in their benediction of it. God has made all things clean,
creation is good. It is from that insight that many of the riches of
Christian history have flowed. It is the impulse behind the

1

elaboration of the sacramental system. The incarnation is the original impulse behind Christian art, architecture, music, calligraphy and every other attempt to claim access to God through the senses. More profoundly, it is this same impulse that is behind the instinct to do justice and seek mercy in Christian history. The incarnation implies a great affirmation of the particular, the specific, the local, the this and that of the universe. Matter is sacramental, instinct with the divine and, when used aright, it is a vehicle of the divine presence, the outward and visible becoming the effective sign of the invisible but real mystery of God.

There is also a redemptive side to the doctrine of incarnation. The Word of God came not just to visit, but 'to visit and redeem' (Luke 1.68). This accounts for the great christological principle enunciated by Gregory of Nazianzus: 'That which has not been assumed is not healed.' In the incarnation, God the creator has blessed and claimed humanity, breaking down every barrier that divides us from the divine and from one another. Christ has opened up a way of free access to God. Of course, the Church has never been absolutely comfortable with this divine liberality and has spent a lot of time in history contradicting and rearranging it. The most eloquent statement of this anxious revisionism in Christian history is found in Dostoevsky's famous parable of the Grand Inquisitor who sends Christ to his death in Seville because humanity cannot bear his terrible gift of freedom and trades it for the security of authoritarian Christianity. The most potent result of this tendency in the history of institutional Christianity, now somewhat diluted by the recovery of a proper theology of the people of God, has been the intense clericalizing of the Church, in all its versions, but particularly in the Catholic tradition. Even so, in spite of these institutionalizing tendencies, the doctrine of the incarnation has acted as a dissolvent of barriers and distinctions. In Christ our flesh is united to God, so our bodies are sacramental, means of grace, not obstacles to it. The doctrine of the incarnation has a profound effect on our attitude to creation, to people and the natural order; but it also has a revolutionary effect on our attitude to ideas, to the whole field of human development.

And this is because the second important implication of the incarnation is that God is known in and through time. Creation is a time-and-place-continuum and both aspects of the continuum are important and inseparable. Just as God is known in thingness and materiality, so God is known and expressed in successiveness, in the movement of time and change. The idea that the divine revelation was confined solely to Palestine in the first forty or fifty years of the Christian era is not what the doctrine of the incarnation is about. That would be a localized epiphany, a showing of God to particular people at a particular time, to which we could only respond today with longing and regret, as we pore over the patchy records of the experience. In fact, incarnation is a much more dynamic and developing reality than that. It is a divine initiative that is still living and active. This means that God is found in and through history, in which the divine purpose continues to unfold. God is God of time, not God of a time warp. The Church cannot be a preservation society, if the doctrine of the incarnation is true. Rooted in the knowledge of God's action in the past, it looks ahead to discern God's action in the future. Under the continuous guiding and prompting of the Holy Spirit, covenanted to be with the Church until the end, the Church is endlessly challenged to reform and renew itself and to discover the depths of God's riches as they unfold in history. So the Church looks to the past and to the future with equal intensity. A Church that looks only to the past, a conservationist Church, denies God's sovereignty over history, time future as well as time past. And a Church that looks only to the future, a progressivist Church, denies the normative nature of the originating event in Palestine. For that event to mean anything to us, to mean something living and active, it must have a continuous reality, a real presence in history. But living as opposed to dead facts are disturbing and unpredictable. This is why the Christian way is a way of painful struggle in the intellectual as well as in the moral sphere.

So the reality of the incarnation has two profound consequences. The first is what is called the sacramental principle, the conviction that the material is mystical. Obviously, this is reflected in the Church in the pattern of sacramental life, in the specific ordinances to which Christ attached a promise, particularly baptism and Eucharist. But behind these foundational sacraments there lies a whole hinterland of what are sometimes called sacramentals, a whole aesthetic of creation. This accounts for the inevitable, though sometimes corrupting, elaborations of Christian worship. This

3

elaborating impulse lies behind many of the glories of Western culture, the instinct to offer to God the best of human genius. But it also involves a whole-hearted commitment to the human enterprise. Theories about the best way to achieve human flourishing vary, but the incarnation of God in human history commits us to the struggle, however we conceive it. One strong tradition in human history is the myth of past perfection in a vanished golden age. People have spent great energy trying to replicate their idea of original perfection. Alternatively, they have spent so much time lamenting the corruption of the present, the decline from some imagined ideal standard, that they have found little energy to address the problems of the day. This is where the second consequence of the incarnation registers its importance, because it summons us to discern God's action in history and co-operate with it. That action is negative as well as positive. It both judges and affirms.

This means that Christians are summoned to a discipline of double discernment, both privately and as they participate in the great developments that constantly accompany human history. One side of that discipline of discernment is the constant task of self-examination, leading to amendment of life. Christians not only confess their sins and receive forgiveness, they seek to co-operate with the work of sanctification which is the action of the Holy Spirit in their lives. Christians are called to lead examined lives. They are not fixed objects but organic beings, called to the perfection of their own nature and therefore engaged inescapably in personal change and development. Unless, of course, as S. T. Coleridge said of William Pitt, they 'were cast, rather than grew'. Certainly, many Christians would boldly confess to and make a virtue of a certain rigidity of character and outlook, but to do so they must ignore the dynamic nature of God's action upon human character and human history. As Cardinal Newman frequently pointed out, growth is the only evidence of life and to grow is to change. And part of that changefulness must be the cumulative discarding of vicious habits and opinions, the repudiating of prejudice and discrimination. This is what Christians mean by repentance, a complex activity that involves discarding wrong attitudes and publicly espousing right ones. It is certainly easier for individuals to do this than for humanity in its collective forms, but institutional repentance for collective or systemic sin can happen and is powerfully effective when it does. There have been several celebrated examples in recent Christian history.

For instance, in 1972 Pope Paul VI repudiated the ancient Christian accusation that the Jews had killed God, the sin of deicide, and thereby publicly repented for centuries of anti-semitism in the Church. An equally dramatic example of public repentance took place in South Africa in 1990, when the Dutch Reformed Church publicly repented the sin of racism and the heresy of apartheid and invited Archbishop Tutu to absolve them. Though deeply tragic, these acts of public repentance and repudiation of past sins are profoundly liberating. They reveal the inner nature of Christian history as a dynamic struggle between human inertia and divine activity. This struggle is the glory and the shame of Christian history. Again and again we are judged by our own gospel, but we are not thereby utterly cast down, for repented sin is sin forgiven. Paul cautions us not to look back at mistakes we have repudiated, but to 'press on toward the goal for the prize of the upward call of God in Christ Jesus' (Phil. 3.13–14). We look back only to put the past behind us, but we can only do that honestly by owning our failures. The power of the past is only robbed of its sting when we repent of it. Thus it was that the Christian community, after centuries of indifference, publicly repented of the great evil of slavery, though there were many Christians who offered their benediction to that monstrous denial of the incarnation. Thus it was that Christians in the USA publicly repented of the sin that denied African Americans their civil rights. And thus it is that many Christian men today are publicly repenting the sin of sexism in themselves and in the Church. They are acknowledging that for centuries the Church has discriminated against women, according them a lower status than men, thereby denying the liberating truth of the incarnation. In a way, this book is a public act of reparation to women for the way their Christian brothers have treated them down the ages.

There are grave charges to answer, as we reflect upon and seek to repent of our past. Indeed, in one of the contributions to this book we examine the charge levelled against Christianity by many post-Christian feminists that Christianity is intrinsically and irredeemably sexist and oppressive to women, put most recently by Daphne Hampson in *Theology and Feminism*. I believe that Iain Torrance effectively answers the charge in this volume, but he takes it very seriously. For many women, alas, we have already been found guilty. For many others, however, the jury is still out. This book is, in one of its aspects, an act of repentance, based on a discerning analysis of Christian history and gospel tradition.

So the incarnational energy of the gospel calls us constantly to acts of judgement, of ourselves and of our institutions, that lead to acts of repentance, to changes of mind and changes of structure. But this is only one side, the negative side, of the work of discernment to which we are called. It is well represented in this book, as we reflect upon the ways, subtle and blatant, in which Christian men have conspired to keep women in the place they have assigned to them, either elevated beyond rationality onto an unearthly pedestal, or kept firmly in the background as pliant subjects of male domination. This is an important confessional activity, but it is not the only element in Christian discernment. Just as important is affirmative discernment. Negative discernment seeks to discover the ways we have offended against God's action in history and in our private lives; affirmative discernment seeks to identify God's new activity, God's prompting of our minds and hearts to receive the truth that is unfolding in Christian history.

Another way to describe this activity of discernment is to see it as prophecy. Prophets, notoriously and famously, denounce the sins of the people; just as importantly, they point to the new paths of righteousness, the new things of God, and encourage their people to walk in them. And prophecy is a permanent characteristic of the Church. Cardinal Newman, following an ancient Christian tradition greatly loved by the Protestant Reformers, found the description of Christ as prophet, priest and king an intensely useful way of understanding Christian history and discerning God's hand in it. The priestly element in Christian history represents the cultic or devotional side of the Church's life, while the kingly role reflects the Church's need to guide its moral and institutional life wisely. But the real passion lies in prophecy and it gets to the heart of Christ's own method. Prophecy opens up to us the burning heart of God, burning with frustrated love at our moral and spiritual feebleness; burning with desire for us to discover the deeper things of God and boldly follow them. It has often been pointed out that prophecy is about forth-telling, not fore-telling. It tells forth the truth revealed by God to minds sensitive to God's teaching. And it always meets with resistance. Any reading of history will substantiate this claim. Moral and spiritual progress is always the result of the prophetic minority challenging the resistant majority. It is this fact that exposes the dubiousness of the claim made by Anglo-Catholic opponents of women's ordination that a decision to ordain women can only be made by the unanimous consensus of Catholic Christianity in a General Council. Even if one were to accept the claim that developments in Christian history have to receive their final seal of acceptance by such a council, history teaches us that it is always the brave and prophetic minority that finds the energy to start the process that ends in conciliar consensus. This is the divine method as revealed in the incarnation, as it was the method of the God of the Old Testament, who was always sending prophets to a stiff-necked generation to call it into the paths of justice. The truth or justice of a claim cannot be established by administrative machinery, no matter how broadly based it is.

This book is not about the ordination of women, though the contributors are all concerned about the issue. Even when women are fully admitted into all the orders of ministry the struggle will not be over, because the underlying problem will not be resolved by an act of administrative reorganization, nor even by an act of institutional repentance. Nevertheless, the current debate about women's ordination provides the most pointed contemporary example of the perennial human struggle between moral justice and institutional inertia. When I am debating the ordination of women with Anglican Catholics I invariably end up by making one point that concentrates on the issue of justice that is at the centre of the debate. There are, of course, many people who are incapable of rational debate on the subject. These are the 'impossibilists', who believe that women are incapable, by nature, of receiving ordination, very much the way a man is incapable of bearing children. For them anatomy is destiny, a theme explored by Michael Jacobs in this book. Facts do not budge this conviction. No amount of exposition of the part society and culture have played in determining male and female roles will move impossibilists to new reflection upon their attitudes. They are reminiscent of the

Richard Holloway

rock-hard convictions of certain racist philosophies that adduce 'scientific' evidence to demonstrate the inferiority of other races. This position is a psychopathology with which it is impossible to argue. The real issues lie buried in the complicated fears and hatreds that have characterized male and female relations for millennia. The acceptable face of this type of immovable prejudice is what is called the ecumenical argument. When applied to the Anglican Church it goes something like this: admittedly, there are no obstacles to, or arguments against, ordaining women that are absolutely valid for all time; nevertheless, such a departure from ancient tradition can only be achieved on the basis of a universal consensus of Catholic Christendom. (People who argue like this automatically assume that churches in the Protestant tradition have nothing to teach us about the matter, or any other matter.) It is at this point I ask my interlocutors if they would accept women's ordination if the Pope signed a paper mandating it tonight. (Most of my friends in the Roman Catholic episcopate tell me they could accept women priests tomorrow if the Pope said it was all right.) If they say that even the Pope could not mandate it, then there is an end to the discussion, but if they agree with most of my Roman Catholic friends who are just waiting for the Pope to give the go-ahead, then there can clearly be no objection in principle to women's ordination, because not even the Pope can make a wrong thing right. If he *could* say that it is all right to do it, then it must already be all right in principle. The only thing that is holding it back is the administrative inertia of institutional Christianity that always takes its time to admit the obvious. (The fact that it took the Pope till 1972 to exonerate the Jews makes the point perfectly. Were the Jews Christ killers till 1972 and innocent thereafter? No, it was the Church that was sinfully wrong till it repented of its sin a mere twenty years ago.) If women *can* be ordained when the Pope makes up his mind to permit it, then it is only the state of the Pope's mind that stands in their way. It is not principle or truth or biological fact. It is simply time, the time it takes to change one man's mind. But if that is already the case, then to deny ordination to women now is already unjust. Once the point of consciousness has been reached that recognizes that there are no longer any *reasons* why a given group may not be admitted to a particular institution, to continue to deny the group access becomes a culpably

8

unjust act. Before the moment of awareness was reached the denial was unjust but not culpable. The oppressor was in a state of ignorance and could not be held responsible for his action. But once the moment of illumination has been achieved, to deny access to the right under dispute on prudential or expedient grounds is no longer a moral or theological calculation. It has become a worldly or institutional one, of the sort that sent Jesus to the cross, because it was better that one man be sent to an unjust death than that the whole nation perish. It is impossible to conceive of Jesus operating within such a sub-moral institutional logic. He belonged to the prophetic tradition that pioneered truth from the front and did not wait for the majority to reach an agreed consensus before taking action.

This book, then, is a thematic treatment of a particular example of human development, prompted by the God who works through history. It is also about the forces that range themselves against this development, forces of fear, confusion and even hatred. But the underlying issue is about the nature of faith itself. In his remarkable book *The Psychology of Military Incompetence* Norman F. Nixon[2] describes the authoritarian personality. Authoritarian personalities (drawn to the armed services for obvious reasons, but also, in my experience, very common in the ordained ministry) have a number of characteristics, but two of them are particularly important. One is a kind of dependent obedience that renders the possessor incapable of challenging authority, even when it is obviously and disastrously wrong. Related to this manifestation of psychological insecurity is the fear of failure. So deep is the fear of making a mistake that this type of person rarely initiates, because fear of failure is a stronger drive than the hope for success or victory. The applications of all this to military history are obvious. Many of the most tragic military disasters have been the result of a lack of daring, an inability to risk, an imprisoning incapacity to try anything new. Behind all this lies a complicated pathology of emotional insecurity, a profound lack of trust in one's own abilities or sense of destiny or good fortune. In fact, behind it all there is a lack of faith. Faith takes risks because it trusts in a graceful God who calls us to the untidy experiment of living and who forgives our mistakes before we make them, as long as we make them in good faith. No one

9

captured faith's creative untidiness better than Dietrich Bonhoeffer. He noted that Christians make their choices boldly, because their confidence 'depends on a God who demands responsible action in a bold venture of faith and who promises forgiveness and consolation to the man who becomes a sinner in that venture'.[3]

Behind the vacillations and timidity of Christian bodies as they respond to the challenge of the women's movement there lies a deep faithlessness that is rooted in a peculiarly male type of insecurity that has to keep things neat and tidy and nailed down, with everything in its place, especially women. The contributors to this book hope they disturb that graveyard fear. We call our brothers to a radical trust in the God who brings us to repentance for our past history of discrimination against women, caused by our unadmitted desire to cling to the privileges of male power, and invites us to discern and embrace the new thing that is being done in our day — the perfecting of the liberty of *all* the children of God.

Notes

1. *Letters* (Longmans, Green & Co. 1944), p. 63.
2. Norman F. Nixon, *The Psychology of Military Incompetence*. Futura.
3. *Letters and Papers from Prison* (SCM 1967), p. 29.

L. WILLIAM COUNTRYMAN

1 *The good news about women and men*

The Christian tradition has come in for criticism, in our time, as being sexist. Some have characterized it as inherently oppressive toward women and think it either beyond reclamation or in need of wholesale reconstruction. Other critics have been more moderate, but still see Christianity as more a part of the problem than of the solution. I shall be suggesting, in what follows, that if we return to the centre of our gospel, we find that sexism is repugnant to Christianity; but I do not mean by this to deny the cogency of the criticisms. The Christian tradition, more often than not, has excluded women from roles of authority and power. It has admitted them to baptism, but denied them full and equal membership in the Church. It has, at times, treated them as intrinsically impure and therefore incapable of drawing near to the holy. Or sometimes, it has distanced them in another way by putting them on a pedestal and asked them to behave as if they were intrinsically pure, remote, spiritual, unapproachable beings. Through much of our history, the tradition has instructed them to redeem themselves by being content with a domestic position that amounted to little better than servitude, giving them little opportunity to escape from it, no matter how grievously they might be abused.

It is important, however, to remember that Christian tradition is not a monolithic, but a composite reality. It is compounded of a great diversity of elements, of which only one, the gospel or good news itself, is truly and finally authoritative for Christians. In addition to this good news, other elements shaping the tradition include: the cultures in which the gospel first appeared and became indigenized (mainly Mediterranean and European, both Jewish and non-Jewish), the institutionalization of the early Christian communities, liturgical development, intellectual extrapolation and codification of basic Christian doctrines, elaborations and ornamentations produced by piety, all sorts of compromises which enabled the Church to survive or retain authority in its environing society.

11

There is a long-standing Christian tendency to treat 'the tradition' as a decisive factor in matters of belief and behaviour. Whether this is a highly formalized doctrine of tradition, as among some Catholics, or the more informal 'We have never done it that way' of some Protestants, tradition is a powerful force among us all. We do not set it aside lightly — and my own predisposition is to think that we should not do so. Tradition, after all, is the ongoing life of the community. Whatever we may claim for it, it is not in fact some pure distillate of the past or of the pure doctrine nor does it give us direct access to the mind of Jesus and the apostles nor is it directly authenticated by the Holy Spirit. What tradition really is (and that is quite important enough) is a community constantly changing without losing its identity. The change, of course, may represent either growth or decay; but it is tradition, either way.

Thus, change is as integral to tradition as continuity. The differences between the second century and the tenth—or the sixteenth or the twentieth—are as much a part of Christian tradition as what they have in common. This means that tradition forces us to make choices; it is open to—indeed, demands of us—criticism as well as applause, reform as well as co-operation. And the composite character of the tradition makes such criticism and reform possible from within, as we can see from other aspects of the life of modern Christianity. The twentieth-century liturgical movement, for example, initiated major reforms in Christian worship precisely by criticizing existing liturgies in the name of principles elicited from earlier ones and from the study of liturgical development. This, in turn, has had a major impact on Christian piety, criticizing the privatism which so often seemed to detach it from the worship of the whole community. The liturgical forms and pious habits which the liturgical movement attacked and the principles by which it attacked them were equally parts of the tradition. The internal complexity of the tradition makes such developments not only possible but, in broad terms, inevitable.

The situation with regard to sexism in the church is similar. If there are elements in the tradition which speak in a sexist way, there are other elements that express the opposite, the principle of full equality of male and female in Christ. The great question is how one can appropriately decide on a starting point. Is one aspect of the tradition, in this case, more authoritative than the other? If so, which side? And why? In addition, is it possible to argue the case in a way that does not merely presume the result? Do we inevitably begin by choosing up sides on the modern issue and then look for prooftexts? Or can we propose a more general process of theological thinking that might guide us in deciding other, similar issues as well?

We must at least *hope* that there are some general principles we can apply and a theological method we can make explicit. If not, we are condemned merely to make factions and shout each other down. 'Liberals' will scorn 'reactionaries' because they are 'close-minded' and cannot 'see' the tradition the liberals see; and 'conservatives' will judge 'radicals' because they are not 'faithful to the tradition' as the conservatives define it. In such a situation, we owe it to the tradition itself, constantly pleading for unity from the New Testament epistles onward, to look for ways of talking with one another—ways that take shared Christian values as the starting point and thereby de-escalate the polemics. While there is no magic shortcut to such a dialogue, it might at least encourage movement in that direction if I make my presuppositions—a quite traditional set of presuppositions, as it turns out—clear at the outset.

I presume, first, that the tradition is of enormous importance and should be deliberately changed only for serious cause. Indeed, it *can* be changed only if there is a substantial consensus accepting the change. Otherwise, the old consensus will reassert itself in other ways. Thus, at the time of the Reformation, a number of Protestant leaders wanted to institute more frequent Communion and tried to force a new consensus in favour of it. The old, contrary consensus, however, prevailed, with the result that the Reformers succeeded only in reducing the number of Eucharists, not in increasing the number of Communions. I believe that the tradition is constantly undergoing change both through the creativity of the community and through unconscious adaptation to changed circumstances; but only the deliberation and assent of the Church as a whole can produce intentional change in the tradition.

Second, I presume that the voice of the faithful is to be heard and that serious discontent on the part of some portion of the faithful is to be taken seriously. Had it been otherwise, the Church as we know it would not exist. From the very beginning, challenges were being raised by those who were in a position of relatively little power in the Church. One thinks, for example, of the challenge by the Hellenists at Jerusalem, who complained that the system of distributing alms was short-changing the widows who belonged to their number (Acts 6.1–6). Had the Twelve reacted merely by reaffirming the tradition of their own leadership, one guesses that the whole Hellenist segment of the community would have been lost. Again, when Gentile Christians from Antioch challenged the Jerusalem authorities for the right to be Christians without becoming Jews, the purely 'traditionalist' response was to reaffirm the existing tradition and require either their full conversion (signalled by circumcision of the males) or their expulsion; but the authorities heeded the petitions of the Gentile faithful, even though it was probably a politically dangerous step and one that they had trouble adhering to in later practice (Acts 15.1–35).

Third, I presume that some values within our tradition are more fundamental than others and that the most fundamental is the good news itself—that message which Jesus preached and lived and which God sealed by raising Jesus from the dead. The heart of that good news, as I understand it, is the proclamation 'You are forgiven'. In this proclamation of good news, God addresses every individual equally. There is no distinction made between Jew and non-Jew, between people of one colour and another, between educated and uneducated, between 'good people' and 'sinners', between male and female. Precisely for this reason, we who have some claim to righteousness have always found it a difficult message. We, the religious, are the older brother of the prodigal son, the workers who bore the heat of the day, the priests and scribes and Pharisees who felt that Jesus was undermining the moral order. We do not want these others made equal with us. But, like it or not, that *was* Jesus' message. Many people, including even some like us, heard it as good news and still do.

If your understanding of the good news is quite different from this, you may not agree with the rest of what I have to say; but at least you will know where we parted company. For the three presuppositions I have named govern and give rise to what follows here. I take the tradition with great seriousness, particularly that very ancient and, indeed, primary aspect of it which we call 'Scripture'. I believe that the church as a whole has a responsibility to listen to all the faithful and not to reject, out of hand, the complaints of the less powerful simply because the tradition, in its current state, does not take them into account. I believe that the gospel is God's word of forgiveness, based not on our own worthiness but on God's unbounded generosity and therefore as valid for my neighbour as for myself and as valid for me as for my neighbour. These three presuppositions have compelled me—at times against my own rather conservative temperament—to take seriously the issue of sexism in the Christian tradition and to see what remedies may be available within the tradition itself.

It is the gospel, I think, which makes sexism untenable for Christians. The present crisis is not, as some complain, a case of 'the world' setting the agenda for the Church. Even if it could be shown that the issue was first raised by 'outsiders', the gospel nonetheless compels us to listen because the charge, if accurate, means that we are behaving inconsistently with the good news. As Christians, we are not free to base our ethos (and therefore our ethics) on a diversity of principles. If we try to do so, we shall end by setting up some rival to the good news, some *law* to which we owe our real loyalty. This was Paul's complaint against the circumcision party—that they were betraying faith in Christ by adding to it a requirement that gentile male Christians be circumcised (Gal. 5.2–12). No doubt they *intended* nothing of the sort, but they were in fact adding something else by way of a precondition for belonging to the Church and thereby they implied that Christ alone is not sufficient for access to God, but only Christ-plus-circumcision. There is no room for such additional requirements in our faith, for if access to God depends on something other than God's forgiveness of us in Christ, then that forgiveness is not sufficient and the good news is false.

This does not mean that the gospel contains nothing that we might call 'law'. If we take 'law' in the common sense of 'directions for living', the gospel certainly does have a law attached to it—or rather growing from it. Jesus summed this law up in two commandments which he selected out of the Torah: love God with your whole self, and love your neighbour as yourself (Mark 12.28–34). These are not incidental, miscellaneous, or idiosyncratic choices; rather, they are the inevitable consequences of the good news. If we truly hear the gospel of forgiveness and apply it

15

to ourselves and our world, the results will be that we love the one who has loved us enough to forgive and that we recognize every other person as being in exactly the relationship with God that we ourselves enjoy. What God has done for each, God has done for all. Knowing this, we can no longer treat our neighbour either as better than ourselves or as worse. Indeed, we must treat the neighbour as another self, so that we cannot love self without loving neighbour nor neighbour without loving self.

Jesus based this law on no extraneous source—not, for example, on Scripture or on creation. According to the record in the gospels, he used to appeal to Scripture in a rather offhand way—sometimes affirming it and sometimes cancelling it. He asserted the superiority of his own message over that of Scripture, even while he also maintained that there was continuity between them (Matt. 5.17–48). According to Mark, the crowds commented on this departure from scribal modes of instruction (Mark 1.22). Let it be granted that the narrative of creation and fall in Genesis 2–3 defines woman as secondary and subordinate to man. Yet, in itself, this does nothing to determine the Christian ethos of male and female. It acquires force for us only if the forgiveness we all, female and male alike, share and the commandments of love derived from it confirm such subordination.

Unfortunately, Christian theologians have repeatedly looked outside the gospel for the authority to make ethical judgements. For example, we have borrowed ideas of 'natural' law from ancient Stoicism, sometimes tricking them out in Hebrew dress; while condemning gnostic antagonism toward the material creation, we have covertly accepted it in the form of ascetic suspicion toward everything bodily; while claiming to honour the biblical teaching of a humanity that is as much body as it is spirit, we have repeatedly swerved toward regarding spirit as sufficient by itself; all too often, we have seen our primary mission as nothing more than justifying the existing standards of our communities. Some aspects of this openness to outside influences may be acceptable. Christianity is not, in practice, an altogether exclusivist tradition. It has been fairly receptive to the whole range of cultural influences it has encountered, whether from Jewish Scripture and midrash or Greek philosophy, from the late-antique *Zeitgeist* or the successive emergent social orders of medieval and modern Europe. These alternative sources of ethical guidance, then, are not necessarily to be rejected out of hand. They may even be permitted to shape the details of Christian life. What we cannot grant them, however, is that they have a right to prevail against the good news itself. If they do so, we are no longer really Christians, whatever label we may be using for ourselves.

The same must be said even with regard to Scripture itself. Not every passage in the New Testament constitutes a direct and immediate proclamation of the good news. Political and social exigencies, as we shall see, sometimes pushed the earliest Christians into compromises for the sake of their community's welfare. It is even possible, as we are told in the story of Jesus' temptation, for the devil to quote Scripture. What we must aim to understand is not just what the Scriptures say (though I do wish, myself, to understand that as exactly and literally as possible) but how they are related to the fundamental thing, the gospel itself. It is quite easy to take a quotation from the New Testament, detach it from all concern about good news and turn it into a new law, a new demand for circumcision, something to be done in addition to accepting the forgiveness offered in Christ. Indeed, we have done it repeatedly. In the second century, Saint Irenaeus contrasted 'the much-speaking of the law' with 'the brevity of faith and love'.[1] Since his time, Christians have repeatedly pasted together their own long-winded law codes and often forgotten to notice that there is a conflict here, that law codes are not the same thing as gospel, that we owe them no ultimate allegiance.

My point, then, is that the gospel is the exclusive foundation for Christian ethics. There is no other foundation for them. No Christian 'law' can have force unless it emerges clearly and persuasively from the good news as its source. With this principle in mind, let us turn now to some specific texts in order to discern what the gospel may have to say about sex as a distinction among human beings, about the relationship of the sexes to one another, and therefore about the proper place of women in the Christian tradition as it moves into its third millennium.

Since I have written elsewhere on the New Testament foundations for sexual ethics (by which I mean not simply rights and wrongs of sexual intercourse, but the whole business of what sex means in human life lived under the good news), I will assume a good deal of that discussion, let it inform my presentation of the issues here, and try to move on into questions especially pertinent to the present topic. If the reader finds some of my statements here surprising or unpersuasive, I refer her or him to the more detailed exegetical arguments I have presented elsewhere.[2] The first thing to say is that sexual issues are treated in Scripture under two broad headings: those having to do with property considerations and those having to do with purity and impurity. Both headings are relevant to the issue of sexism in Christianity today. Under 'property considerations', I include the whole range of family and social issues, such as divorce, the social status of women, the right of women to function in society (including the Church) on an equal footing with men. Under 'purity', I include a range of issues having to do with access to the sacred and the relative religious acceptability of different kinds of people.

The property issues, since they are at least superficially easier for us modern people to grasp, will make a good starting point. In the ancient Mediterranean world, the family (or, more exactly, the household, including slaves and freed persons) was the basic social unit and individuals found a secure place in society only as expressions or instruments of the life of the household. Men and women had sharply contrasting roles in this regard, the man serving both practically and symbolically as the household's interface with the larger society, the woman as the embodiment and focus of the household's inner life. As students of the classics know, the lives of men tended to focus on the agora (or its Israelite equivalent, the city gate), the lives of women on the house itself. Family 'togetherness', so much a part of some modern middle-class ideals, was not a major element in the family expectations of antiquity.

Men and women, then inhabited largely separate spheres. As in the modern experience of racial segregation or apartheid, 'separate' also meant 'unequal'. As daughters, women were of value to their natal family largely as virgins who could be married off to effect alliances with other families. As wives, they were of value to their husband's family (which never became truly their own) as producers of heirs, managers of the household, and part of the domestic workforce. They were, most likely, not entirely without voice in family decisions; but they had little or no legal recourse and were not likely to receive social support, even from their natal family, if they were perceived as insubordinate. Only widowhood might bring a measure of independence—and that only if the woman had produced a male heir; otherwise, she might merely be sent back to her father's house. The woman, then, was a kind of property, first of her father and then of her husband. While both men and women existed for the good of the ongoing family, the woman was relatively less free than her brother. She was an instrument of family statecraft and was attached essentially to the private sphere.

Jesus seems to have interfered with or violated these social and cultural presuppositions in several ways during his ministry. For one thing, he allowed women among his disciples. While it seems to have been the rule that Jewish religious teachers should not speak with women in public, he felt no difficulty about doing so. It appears that a group of women even accompanied him and his male disciples on their travels (Luke 8.1–3). In one well-known story, he is represented as defending one such female disciple from her sister's demand that she return to more familiar female roles (Luke 10.38–42). All this suggests that Jesus treated his female disciples much like the male ones. He demanded of both that they make a sharp break from their families if they wished to join his inner circle. Just as a limited number of men responded to this challenge and left their homes and families to follow him, so did a number of women. If the women were fewer in number, that is less surprising than that they existed at all.

The story of the woman at the well in the Fourth Gospel captures the ambiguity occasioned by Jesus' behaviour (John 4.1–42). That he should even speak to a strange woman was bad enough. That she was a Samaritan made the matter worse. But even beyond that, she proved to be essentially *déclassé*, a kind of 'failed' woman who had had an excessive number of husbands and now lived with a man who had no formal responsibility for her. Jesus' conversation with her is often interpreted as 'convicting' her of her sinfulness. Yet, there is no suggestion of that in the text itself. The woman merely changes the subject (perhaps a sign of embarrassment, but hardly of contrition) and, later, marvels over the stranger's intimate knowledge of her past. Surely, the significant thing about this woman was that she was a free agent, no longer a subordinate part of a family. That made her an ideal disciple from the perspective of a Jesus who, the synoptics tell us, was consistently demanding separation from family (e.g., Mark 10.23–31). And, in fact, her ministry proved far more fruitful than that of the suspicious male disciples in Jesus' immediate entourage.

Jesus not only encouraged both men and women to desert their families. He tried to reshape the marriage bond itself by prohibiting divorce. Later interpretation has often seen this as a kind of intensification of the law or a hardening of discipline for Christians—the setting up of 'higher' standards. The narrative in Matthew 19.1–12, interestingly enough, suggests that it may actually have been meant to make marriage less advantageous for men. The reason is easy enough to understand. A man's family contracted a marriage for him in order to continue the life of the family. His own sexual satisfaction would be one result of it, but it was not the family's primary concern. On the whole, divorce was a remedy not for sexual or personal incompatibility, as in the twentieth-century West. It was a remedy rather for the groom's family, the primary contractual agent, in situations where the bride failed to produce an heir or where the possibility of another, more desirable alliance appeared on the horizon. The bride, after all, was essentially a kind of property for which the family had contracted and who could be disposed of if the family needed or found a better way to achieve its goals.

By prohibiting divorce, Jesus transformed the status of the wife from that of disposable property acquired for the family's advantage to that of permanent member of the husband's family. No doubt, the transformation was not instantaneous or complete. Few things are more difficult for us to change than our notion of what the family is or is not. Americans, for example, have found it very difficult to adapt to the reality that most of our 'families' now follow non-traditional patterns such as single-parent households or the amalgamation of distinct families through divorce and remarriage or through gay or lesbian partnerships with children from previous marriages. Many of us simply do not see these as 'families', since they do not correspond to our familiar pattern of a married couple with their biological children. In the same way, one suspects that many ancient Christians accepted the permanence of marriage simply as a new law or as an ideal to be aimed at and never noticed that it implied a radically changed status for the wife. Yet, the implication was there, as Matthew skilfully underlined in his reporting of the matter.

Yet, one might ask why, if Jesus really regarded women as full equals to men in discipleship and tried to put them on an equal footing with their husbands, he did not include any women in the number of the Twelve. This omission is sometimes urged as a reason to continue excluding women from full and equal membership in the Church today—particularly from equal access to the sacramental rite of ordination. The argument is an awkward one for a variety of reasons. For example, does the omission of Gentile males from among Jesus' disciples imply that Gentiles should continue to be excluded from ordination—or even from baptism? One could make a better argument for this than for the exclusion of women as such, for women clearly *were* numbered among the inner circle of those who travelled with Jesus and heard his teaching. The argument is awkward also because it makes the improbable assumption that Jesus created the Twelve as a way of inaugurating the later, settled, localized ministry of the Church. In actuality, the tasks given to the Twelve, according to the Gospels, suggest rather that their primary role was not administration of community life (something they happily surrender to the Seven in Acts 6.2), but itinerant proclamation. It is precisely for this reason that they were all male, since only males could normally gain access to a public hearing among strangers in the town gate or market place. Mary Magdalene could be 'apostle to the apostles' on the first Easter and the Samaritan woman could convert her own townsfolk because a woman *could* gain a hearing within her own community; but to strangers, given the culture of the time, men could most readily serve the function of proclamation.[3]

In sum, we will best understand Jesus' attitude toward women if we interpret him as making the fewest distinctions social expectation would tolerate between the two sexes. Given his desire to see his message spread in public by human representatives rather than by written word, the culture of the time compelled him to assign some functions primarily to men. He subverted the prevailing customs, however, by welcoming women among his disciples, by giving the wife equal status in marriage with her husband, and by calling all of his inner circle, both female and male, to separate themselves from their families and wander the countryside with him. All of this is in full accord with the message that he was proclaiming. God's favour, he insisted, was not dependent on earthly status, whether on the goodness of the devout Pharisee or the merit of the reliable older brother or of the hard-working labourer or the social superiority of male to female. God's favour is the result of God's own act of forgiveness. Therefore each individual is the same as every other in God's eyes, and there can be no ultimate distinction between male and female. We who have heard and believed this good news will respond by wholeheartedly loving the God who has forgiven us and by loving our neighbours, female or male, as forgiven selves in precisely the same sense we are.

From an early time, Christians seem to have had uncertainties and disagreements about how they would put this reality into practice.[4] Women were full and active members in the community from the start, serving as patrons (e.g., Lydia), prophets (e.g., the daughters of Philip), deacons (e.g., Phoebe), apostles (e.g., Junia). Early baptismal teaching acknowledged that baptism brought an end to the distinction between male and female—as to all other social distinctions (Gal. 3.27–9). Women were evidently part of the group visited by the gift of the Spirit on Pentecost (Acts 2.1–4). They were held responsible for their actions in precisely the same degree as their husbands, as the story of Ananias and Sapphira shows (Acts 5.1–11). Yet, there is evidence in our documents that, over the first two centuries, they were shouldered out of leadership in the community. Luke–Acts can be read either as affirming or as diminishing the role of women in the Church.[5] And we find Christian writers (presumably male) who tried to reinforce the subordination of women within the household and within the Church itself.

The existence of exhortations in favour of conventional ancient Mediterranean family mores suggests that early Christian practice had actually been less than conventional. No doubt, the tendency of Christian women to regard themselves as their husbands' equals was one of the criticisms being flung at the new religious community. Indeed, some of the 'traditionalizing' texts tell us explicitly that they are motivated by a concern for what outsiders might think. 1 Peter introduces its 'table of household duties' by telling the hearers that they should avoid antagonizing outsiders and by advocating the most conservative behaviour possible in all areas of life (2.11–17). 1 Timothy restricts the role of women at the church assembly in favour of that of men (2.1–15) and directs that only men are to be placed in leadership—and only heads of household with good public reputations at that (3.1–13). Anxiety about public disapproval and the possibility that it might lead to persecution pushed the Church to retreat from the freedom that Jesus had allowed to his female disciples. Yet another motive for reinstituting subordination of women was the threat of an anti-body asceticism which attacked the household and other expressions of sexuality as a way of opposing belief in God as Creator. Paul countered this threat in 1 Corinthians 7 without abandoning the principle of equality within marriage; but a simple reaffirmation of marriage and family in their familiar form must have seemed an easier expedient. This is evident in Colossians, where the household code of 3.18–4.1 is associated not only with anxiety about the opinions of outsiders (4.5), but with an effort to counter a kind of quasi-Jewish, quasi-Gnostic ascetical teaching (2.8–23).

For Christian ethics in any era and on any subject, a sharp distinction must be drawn between various types of New Testament and traditional precedents. These precedents have a certain authority in and of themselves—an authority which gives them the right to receive a careful, attentive, respectful, and reflective hearing. We must understand, however, that in no era—not even in the first century—is the Church able simply to incarnate the gospel purely, wholly, and without fault into a set of clear-cut and infallible rules for living. In every era, the Christian community lives at the focus of a variety of pressures, social, cultural, and political, which affect our understanding of the good news and which limit our ability to realize it effectively in our lives. It is not appropriate for Christians living in secular societies with freedom of religion to look down on our forebears, living under threat of persecution, and to scorn them for their compromises. On the other hand, neither is it appropriate to perpetuate those compromises when they are no longer necessary. If we want the New Testament to support and inform our ethical

L. William Countryman

analysis today, we must be constantly and consciously seeking for the gospel that lies behind the text. It is not enough to quote texts that support our position; in any case, the New Testament provides texts for all our existing factions, with the net result that they merely cancel one another out. Only by moving through the texts to the gospel can we hope to reach agreement or, if worse comes to worst, to find out exactly where our irremediable disagreements lie.

The gospel, as I have come to understand it through my own life and study and as I am presupposing it in this essay—the gospel knows nothing of any difference of status between women and men. Women are no longer property of their own families or their husbands'. Women are no longer categorically assigned to the private sphere. Women have the same access to discipleship. Women are neither more nor less qualified for public roles in Church and society than men are—unless perhaps by the usage of a particular culture which may make it difficult for their voices to be heard publicly in a given time and place. (Even then, one result of the proclamation of the good news, however many millennia it may take, will be to break down that cultural barrier.)

The modern West has made strides, matched to a degree in other parts of the world, in setting aside the older property ethic in relation to women and in providing for equality of status. While full equality of women may not yet be a fact in many places, it is increasingly seen as a legislative and legal norm and there have been outstanding political gains over the last two centuries. One is compelled, then, to ask why the Church has lagged so far behind the society as a whole. Even if no one saw the equality of women as *commanded* by the gospel, the traditional property ethics would not seem so difficult to abandon. Indeed, most Western Christians have abandoned them willingly enough in the realms of law and public life without any sense of their religion being violated thereby. What is it, then, that makes many Christians so hesitant to admit women to full equality within the Church itself, especially where that involves ordination of women to sacred ministries?

Here, I think, we must turn to the ethic of purity for our answer. But be forewarned that no area of ethics is more difficult for most people to think about or discuss, for purity involves feelings and

24

presuppositions so deep-seated for most of us that they are, initially at least, almost beyond reasoning with. In every culture, people learn to divide their world between clean and unclean, pure and impure; and we typically learn this very early in life—so early that we have no recollection of having learned it at all. As a result of the broad agreement among people of our own culture on the question of what is pure or impure and of our having no consciousness that these distinctions were learned ones, we are quite likely to think and, more importantly, feel that these are simply universal human givens. Yet, in reality, as early modern travellers and more recent anthropologists have so amply documented, no two cultures have identical definitions of purity. The basic notion of clean and dirty may be a human universal, but the exact description of what belongs in either category is culturally determined. Sometimes it bears a relationship to hygiene—but not always. In any case, our cultural concern with purity goes far beyond hygiene to regulate all sorts of human activities, particularly in connection with religion.

We can recognize purity responses in ourselves by the element of disgust or, more intensely, revulsion which characterizes them. In English-speaking societies, this is perhaps clearest in reactions to male homosexual acts, which apparently violate our most emphatic purity taboo. Most people, in my experience, can offer no very coherent reason why these acts should be construed as wrong. When reasons are offered, they often prove to be factually erroneous or, at the least, unexamined. The suspicion, for example, that gay men are particularly likely to molest children is unfounded—indeed, contradicted by the available data. Or the common claim that their sexual acts are 'unnatural' usually turns out to be unclear or insubstantial, since there is no consensus in our culture as to what we mean by 'natural' or 'unnatural'—and by our most common definitions, homosexual acts are, in fact, quite natural. Yet, there often goes along with the rejection of such acts a kind of visceral revulsion which makes the lack of substantive ethical reasoning seem irrelevant to many people. This is a purity code in operation.

I do not mean to be saying that purity codes are either bad or good in themselves. They simply are. No society is without them. It is important, however, to understand that they affect us

25

differently from other kinds of ethics. Purity ethics tend to be less open to analysis, examination and explanation. Take, for example, the case of rape. Most Christians would have no difficulty giving a coherent and tenable account of why rape is wrong (though, interestingly enough, the Scriptures have almost nothing to say against it). It is wrong because it is an act of violence depriving a person of her (or sometimes his) rightful freedom to govern her (or his) own body. My own response to a case of rape is also filled with revulsion, as it violates the particular purity code which I absorbed from my family and culture. Yet, my reaction is not based solely on this purity ethic; the other ethic, dealing with the use of force, enables me not only to feel, but to explain why I think rape is wrong. Furthermore, I can easily relate the ethic that forbids such use of force to the commandment that I love my neighbour as myself, whereas I cannot readily relate the purity ethic to it. This fact marks rape as a violation of love itself, as contrasted with homosexual acts, which (if not violent, fraudulent, etc.) appear to me to violate only our purity ethic and not the love of neighbour.

Now, one further important thing about purity is that, in our culture as in many others, purity is intimately connected with access to God. Historically, cleanliness (in the sense of purity ethics rather than hygiene) really has been next to godliness for Christians—in fact, it has been the gateway into godliness. And, interestingly, from an early time, the purity in question has been defined largely in sexual terms. Many Christians, from the second century onward, taught and believed that virginity was necessary to salvation—or, at least, to any kind of real seriousness about Christian religion. This was confirmed by the rise of monasticism and, in the medieval West, by the requirement that ordained men be celibate. The laity, as sexual persons, were not to approach the mysteries of word or sacrament too closely. The Reformation removed this barrier to a degree by asserting that marriage was at least equal (or, for some Reformers, superior) to celibacy. Yet, long-standing Christian anxiety about sex as intrinsically impure did not vanish; it merely took on new forms within the reformed traditions.

Where do women fit into all this? A full account must probably come from the pen of an historian[6] rather than a biblical scholar, but a few elements seem clear. Ancient Israelite purity codes have remained significant for Christians by being enshrined in the Scriptures, chiefly Leviticus. While few Christians have accepted them *in toto*, elements of them have found a place in later Christian purity codes, particularly those elements concerned with sex. As I have noted, the general Christian purity code which began to emerge in the second century was concerned, above all, with sex. One element of the Israelite purity code which eventually carried over was disgust at homosexual acts between men. Another was an overall sense that women are intrinsically less pure than men (which may also lie at the base of antagonism toward homosexual acts between men, since one of the men might be seen as being feminized). Women's impurity is manifest, for Leviticus, in menstruation and in childbirth; and one finds both anxieties gradually creeping into later Christian practice, with women barred from receiving Communion during their menstrual periods and requiring 'purification' after childbirth. Thus, both single and married women were automatically suspect of impurity. It was an easy step from that to feeling that they must be kept well away from the altar. The result is an ongoing sense among many Christians that ordination of women simply 'feels wrong'. It is typically a visceral reaction more than an intellectual one.

Now, supposing it be granted that a purity issue is involved here, what if anything does the gospel tell us about the role of purity in Christianity? The answer, I believe, is simple and straightforward. It tells us that purity is irrelevant. No one gains access to God through keeping pure; no one is shut out from God by failing to do so. The issue was a very live one in Jesus' own day. Sects of pious Jews were seeking to define true Judaism in their own image. In the process, each sect scorned and, where possible, disenfranchised all who disagreed with it. Jesus, by contrast, sought his disciples from among all sorts of Jews, from the least to the most pure, and brought them together with one another not on the basis of purity but on the basis of his own authoritative message of forgiveness. His way of teaching and ministering implied that access to God was no longer through the Temple or the Torah (both foci of purity), but through him and the gospel of forgiveness. His resurrection proved to his followers that he was right.

L. William Countryman

Jesus' own indifference to purity became manifest in many ways. He ate with tax-collectors, notorious for their carelessness about food purity. (Food purity appears to have been the focal issue for ancient Jews, much as sex came to be for later Christians.) He allowed a woman made chronically impure by a haemorrhage to touch him and then singled her out for praise rather than blame (Mark 5.25–34). He touched lepers in 'cleansing' (not healing!) them and even risked the most virulent sort of impurity, corpse-uncleanness, on a couple of occasions (Mark 5.41; Luke 7.14). In his teaching, he rejected the importance of physical cleanliness or purity, strongly as it had been emphasized by Leviticus or by contemporary Jewish teachers, and substituted for it the metaphorical idea of a 'purity of the heart', which, for all practical purposes, appears to be precisely equal to the commandment to love neighbour and self alike (Mark 7.14–23).

This is not to say—and it would be mistaken to say—that Jesus forbade the observance of purity ethics. He did not forbid them, but set them aside as irrelevant to the whole question of who gets access to God and how. We have access to God because God has created this access in forgiving us, not because we have avoided pork, menstrual fluids, lepers, corpses or other defiling things. In thanks for the access God has granted us, we respond not by adopting new purity rules, but by loving God and by loving neighbour and self alike. There is nothing in any of this to justify a purity rule which says that women need to be kept further away from the mysteries than men. (Nor, for that matter, is there anything to say that homosexual people should be kept further away than heterosexual ones.)

The individual believer, to be sure, is allowed to continue practising his or her own purity code—but not to inflict it on others or to divide the Church over it. This is an issue that became particularly critical in the time of Paul, when Gentiles had been admitted to the Church on an equal footing with Jews, creating grave problems for those Jews who were committed to a careful observance of purity. Since the non-Jewish Christians were not committed to observing the Levitical purity code (and might not even know it in any detail), Jewish Christians were constantly threatened with contracting impurity as a result of their co-religionists' ignorance or carelessness. Some Gentile Christians,

28

on the other hand, were apparently contemptuous (as many non-Christian Gentiles were) of the punctiliousness of Jews with regard to food purity. They were perhaps inclined to create problems even beyond the inevitable ones. Paul's response was to reprove both groups. He told the punctilious not to judge the careless and the careless not to be contemptuous of the punctilious (Rom. 14.1–4). At the same time, he insisted that, in principle, nothing is really unclean in and of itself; that is to say, no physical impurity can really separate a person from God (14.14). He acknowledged that the person who *fears* that impurity will separate from God must indeed avoid it — because whatever does not proceed from faith is sin (14.14, 23). But that is a matter of the individual conscience and not to be imposed on others.

Where does this leave us with regard to sexism in the Church today? If there are legitimate reasons for a Christian ethos where women are relegated to second-class status simply for being women, I have not yet seen them stated. Being, as I have said above, of a conservative temperament, I should have been happy to see some good reasons, during the long debate in the American Church, not to change the existing form of our tradition. I am convinced, however, that the objection to the ordination of women is, at bottom, a purity objection. This is hardly surprising. Where would such a visceral reaction be more likely to appear than at the altar itself? When our inherited sense of women's greater impurity (a sense shared by many women as well as men) comes into conflict with our most profound assurance of being in God's presence, many of us will necessarily feel far-reaching anxiety. I do not mean to mock that reaction, for it is powerful and real. Yet, I can find no warrant whatever in the gospel for making purity ethics determinative for the life of the Christian community. Just the opposite; we are specifically debarred from doing so. The individual believer is free to follow a purity code which her or his own conscience demands, as long as it does not mean dividing the Church or treating others in a judgemental way. Perhaps those whose purity code is violated by women priests could refrain from receiving Communion at their hands as long as they can do so without creating scandal or schism. In any case, Paul's ruling implies that they should refrain from imposing their purity code on those who do not share it.

L. William Countryman

In the last analysis, the status of women within the Church turns out to be a central issue for our time. On its correct resolution (and that of some related issues) depends our whole grasp of what the gospel means for us—or, more exactly, our understanding of the way the gospel has grasped us. Access to God is not by purity—our own or that of anyone else—but by Jesus Christ and the message of good news which he taught and lived. Nor is any distinction made on a basis of social status. The good news falls upon all equally, Jew or non-Jew, female or male. It transforms us all alike. It summons all alike to love both the Forgiver and the forgiven. Any distinction made by the Church between Jew and Greek or between male and female is gratuitous and in danger of subverting the gospel. This is not to sit in judgement on the accommodations made by early Christians under threat of persecution or the pressure of their immediate cultural presuppositions. They have their judge, the same who will judge us; and may we all alike find mercy. Yet, in a day when historic changes free us to seek a fuller, more adequate incarnation of the good news in the ethos of the Church, we cannot excuse ourselves by appealing to their precedent. Only the gospel itself can give us direction, and its direction is clear. We should be ashamed to be found wanting in our own day.[7]

Notes

1. Irenaeus, *Demonstration of the Apostolic Doctrine*, 87.
2. L. William Countryman, *Dirt, Greed, and Sex: Sexual Ethics in the New Testament and their Implications for Today* (Philadelphia, Fortress Press, 1988; London, SCM Press, 1989).
3. We should not be surprised, however, if women were actually regarded as apostles—perhaps speaking especially (but not necessarily exclusively) to other women, to whom men had little access. Compare the case of Junia (a more likely interpretation than 'Junias') in Rom. 16.7. Compare also such figures in early Christian narrative as Thecla.
4. L. William Countryman, 'Christian Equality and the Early Catholic Episcopate', *Anglican Theological Review* 63 (1981), pp. 115–38. For a more positive reading of the evidence, see Elisabeth Schüssler Fiorenza, *In Memory of Her* (New York, Crossroad, 1985).
5. Cf. Mary Rose D'Angelo, 'Women in Luke–Acts: A Redactional View', *Journal of Biblical Literature* 109 (1990), pp. 441–61.
6. For the early period, we now have important and relatively comprehensive works by Aline Rousselle, *Porneia* (Oxford, Basil

30

Blackwell, 1988), and Peter Brown, *The Body and Society* (New York, Columbia University Press, 1988). For more recent times, one valuable contribution is *Intimate Matters: A History of Sexuality in America* by John D'Emilio and Estelle B. Freedman (New York, Harper & Row, 1988).
7. My thanks to my colleague Rebecca Lyman, from whose critique of this essay I profited greatly.

STEPHEN C. BARTON

2 *Women, Jesus and the Gospels*

I. INTRODUCTION

The aim of this essay is to give *a Christian theological reading* of the stories about women and Jesus in the canonical Gospels.[1] I put it this way because it is very important to clarify our starting-point. First, as a contribution to a book written by men to oppose sexism in the Church, I wish to acknowledge openly that this essay springs from my own commitment, experience, learning and teaching within the fellowship of the Church. I make no pretence at 'pure objectivity' and 'detachment', for the Christian gospel, in all its particularity, is a call to follow the way of God revealed in Jesus in the power of God's Spirit. This does *not* mean that 'anything goes' as a legitimate reading. On the contrary, it means that our concern to give a fair and responsible — even *obedient* — reading of the Gospels will be all the greater. This is what I mean by calling what follows a *Christian* reading.

Second, my primary concern is not that of the ancient historian. This is not to say that historical information is not important: just that its importance is limited. Unless the story from the past is *interpreted* in a way which shows its meaning for the present and the future, it remains stuck in the past as something of antiquarian value only. This applies also to the story of Jesus in his dealings with the women and men of his time. The narrowly historical question, 'What was Jesus' attitude to women?', invites the devastating response, 'So what? What does that have to do with what's happening to us now?' There is a danger, in other words, that this narrowly historical question will *trivialize* both Jesus and women. It will trivialize Jesus by treating him as a Plato or a Seneca or a Musonius Rufus, whereas, for Christians, Jesus is the Christ of God who ushers in the kingdom of God. It will trivialize women by treating them merely as a subject of contemplation by a male figure of the past, rather than as people in their own right who share to the full in the story of redemption in Christ.

The gospel stories about women and Jesus will *speak to us as believers* to the extent that they bear witness to God-in-Christ and to the breaking in to human relations of the kingdom of God. It is theology, Christology and soteriology which will be normative for the believer, not bare history taken on its own. This is why Jane Williams perceptively says:

> . . . the debate about the ministry of women cannot really be carried out along the lines of a debit and credit column: 'Jesus was certainly a man, but, on the other hand, he thought women were important; Jesus did not choose women to be part of the Twelve, but, on the other hand, he *did* choose them to be the first witnesses of the resurrection', and so on. It is not even any good to be able to demonstrate that Jesus was unusually good to women by the standards of his day . . .[2]

This drives the point home strongly: and it is why I have called this essay a *theological* reading rather than a purely historical one.

Nevertheless, this does not mean that there is no point in asking historical questions about Jesus and about the roles, status, etc. of women in the first century, nor historical and literary questions about the Gospels. At the very least, such questions can throw up information of a kind which functions as a basic bench-marker. For example, if it could be shown that the teaching of Jesus was irredeemably sexist, that he systematically discriminated against women *per se*, that women were able to respond to Jesus in only hostile ways, and that the qualities for leadership in the early Christian movement were specific to the male sex only, this would constitute a serious problem for those in the Church today who wish discrimination against women to end. That there is little such evidence is an encouragement to those in favour of women's liberation that they are on the right lines in the way they are interpreting the kingdom of God. So historical evidence can be important, even if only up to a point. It is a question of deciding, as Leslie Houlden points out, 'what arguments are good for what'.[3]

It is important, however, to claim neither too much nor too little for historical investigation. The tendency of conservatives in theology is to claim too much, to *stretch history* in such a way that the past becomes normative for the present without further ado. On this view, once we know 'the attitude of Jesus (or Paul or the author of the Pastoral Epistles) towards women', we know what is to be the place of women in church and society today. (Notoriously, the 'we' here are mostly men!) Theological liberals, on the other hand, tend to claim too little, to *so emphasize the 'gap'* between the present and the past that it becomes difficult for the past—even the past of Jesus—to speak, still, today. If the danger of the conservative approach is to make the present captive to the past, the danger of the liberal approach is to make the past captive to the present.[4]

Interestingly, this tendency to claim either too much or too little for history is a problem in some *Christian feminist writing* as well. Those who (in my view) claim too much for history have a tendency to see Jesus as a first century 'feminist'[5] who taught and practised a 'discipleship of equals'[6] and sought to bring liberation from oppressive patriarchal structures. Problematic here is the proneness of this approach to special pleading on behalf of Jesus and earliest Christianity over against subsequent (especially post-Pauline) developments, when the patriarchal rot set in. Unfortunate also is the tendency for Judaism, and in particular the treatment of women in Judaism, to become the whipping-boy in this kind of approach, because the roots of sexism in Christianity are traced commonly to 'the Jewish background'.[7] Those, on the other hand, who claim too little for history tend to see the entire Christian tradition as so androcentric as to be irredeemable and unredeeming.[8] The effect of this is to cut women (and men) off from the past, from the Church, and from the biblical tradition of liberation. Paradoxically, also, it denies the experience of many women themselves.[9]

This brings me to my third, and final, point. What we need instead is a way of reading the gospel stories about women and Jesus which sees them, neither as normative history (which is to claim too much) nor as mere history (which is to claim too little), but as *Christian Scripture.*[10] This means that we take the Gospels with full religious seriousness as foundation elements of our Christian tradition which have a privileged status for us because the Church has found them to express something fundamental about the character and will of God. By referring to them as Scripture, we are signalling that the Gospels are texts whose quality of 'sacred persistence'[11] means that they transcend the category 'history' and become the basis for a trustful exegesis in which theologically-informed faith, reason, experience and imagination enable their fruitful interpretation and appropriation in the Church today. It also suggests, precisely because we are approaching the Gospels as Scripture, that literary methods of appreciating the stories are at least as important as historical methods. This is why I have described my approach as a theological *reading* of the Gospel stories, as distinct from a kind of literary archaeological dig.

II. THE WITNESS OF MATTHEW

Like all the Gospels, the Gospel of Matthew is a witness to the fulfilment of God's saving work in the life, death and resurrection of the Son of God, Jesus. With the coming of Jesus, 'the kingdom of heaven is at hand' (3.2; 4.17); and Matthew seeks to express what it means to be citizens of this heavenly kingdom, what it means to be God's new people, the Church. Theology, Christology, ecclesiology and ethics are linked inextricably together and provide the framework for understanding what Matthew has to say about the discipleship of women and men.

1. We need to emphasize from the start that, for Matthew, the over-riding reality is the breaking in of the kingdom *of heaven*. This is enormously important. It means that salvation has come: because to speak of heaven is to speak of God and the rule of God. It also means that judgement has come. Social, cultural, political and religious structures, human behaviour and relations between men and women, all are judged in relation to the severe and demanding standards of the kingdom of heaven. 'Heaven', for Matthew, is not 'pie in the sky when you die': it is the presence of God now and in the future in salvation and judgement. I say 'in the future' because the kingdom of heaven is an *eschatological* reality, for Matthew. It concerns, not just the past and the present from the perspective of God, but the future under God, as well. This means that repentance and conversion can never be a static, once-for-all thing, and that human relations of superordination and subordination (including relations between women and men) can ever only be provisional, open always to new revelations of divine wisdom (cf. 11.25–30).

2. Jesus is of pre-eminent importance because he embodies the divine presence and the divine wisdom: '"his name shall be called

35

Emmanuel" (which means, God with us)' (1.23; cf. 28.20). That is why he is called God's *Son*. Sonship, for Matthew (as for the New Testament writers as a whole), is a *metaphor of close relationship* taken over from the Old Testament and Judaism,[12] a relationship of a theological and moral kind, not necessarily contingent upon biological filiation at all. Jesus is God's Son because he is *obedient* to God. He shows this throughout his life and especially at the times of great testing: the temptation in the wilderness (where we note the repeated, 'If you are the Son of God . . .', in 4.1–11), and the garden of Gethsemane (where Jesus prays three times, 'My Father . . . thy will be done'; 26.36–46). Just as God is portrayed as the Father, so Jesus is the Son. But, again, 'Father' and 'Son' here, describe, not a relationship of biological paternity and filiation, but a relationship which is to be understood theologically. The fact that God is *unlike* human fathers is made quite clear: God is 'Our Father *who art in heaven*' (6.9). This is not to deny that this metaphorical language comes from a patriarchal culture and tradition. What I would deny is the suggestion that this language can only be understood in a way which legitimates patriarchal domination. In fact, Matthew's Gospel provides striking evidence to the contrary, in a saying of Jesus specifically addressing the issue of authority relations in the Christian fellowship (23.8–12). What is so noticeable in this saying, is the critique of patriarchal authority relations, the encouragement of an ethos of mutual acceptance and concern, and the pre-eminence given to an ethic of humility:

> But you are not to be called rabbi, for you have one teacher, and you are all brethren. And call no man your father on earth, for you have one Father who is in heaven. Neither be called masters, for you have one master, the Christ. He who is greatest among you shall be your servant; whoever exalts himself will be humbled, and whoever humbles himself will be exalted.

3. The impact of the coming of Jesus as the one who proclaims the kingdom of heaven is evident throughout Matthew's story. Above all, perhaps, the coming of Jesus is presented as *an act of divine grace for all humankind*. For Jesus, the faithful Son, gives his life to atone for the sins of the people and makes possible, thereby, the bringing into being of God's new covenant people

(26.26–9). Women, significantly, figure in important ways in this presentation.

First, there are the four women in the genealogy (1.1–17): Tamar, Rahab, Ruth and 'the wife of Uriah' (i.e. Bathsheba). Their presence in the list is surprising. As Raymond Brown shows, they signify the unexpected and gracious intervention of God through women to overcome human obstacles and bring his purposes to fulfilment: 'It is the combination of the scandalous or irregular union and of divine intervention through the woman that explains best Matthew's choice in the genealogy.'[13] So they foreshadow the role of Mary. In so far as they are all Gentiles (or, as in Bathsheba's case, the wife of a Gentile), they may foreshadow also the inclusion of Gentiles in the people of God which the coming of the Messiah makes possible.

Second, that women share in prominent ways in salvation history is evident also in the role of Mary. For, according to Matthew, a great miracle is worked in her (in fulfilment of biblical prophecy, 1.23); and, in a quite unique way, she is blessed with the presence of God: 'she was found to be with child of the Holy Spirit' (1.18, 20). Noteworthy too is the way in which Mary is made to share so closely the fate of the infant Messiah: both his exaltation (2.11) and his vulnerability and persecution (2.13, 14, 20, 21). In sharing so closely in Jesus' persecution, she proves herself to be a true and exemplary heir of the kingdom of heaven (see 5.10).

Third, women as well as men constitute 'the crowds' who hear the gracious and demanding teaching from Jesus about the will of God. There is very little in the Sermon on the Mount relevant only to men, and what there is can properly be seen as intended, at points, to ameliorate oppressive man–woman relations (e.g. 5.27–30, 31–2). It is important to emphasize the fact that, in a world in which piety is often graded according to gender, and societies of men cut themselves off from women as a way of safeguarding holiness or the quest for wisdom,[14] Jesus teaches in public both men and women, and includes women among his disciples (12.49–50).

Fourth, women as well as men benefit from Jesus' miracles of healing (4.23ff.; 8.14–17; 9.18–26; 9.35ff.; 11.4–5; etc.) and feeding (14.21; 15.38). Matthew's version of the healing of the

Stephen C. Barton

Syrophoenician woman's daughter (15.21–8 par. Mark 7.24–30)
is especially noteworthy. In Matthew, the woman is a 'Canaanite',
an Old Testament expression denoting a Gentile. In the spirit of
the Sermon on the Mount (at 5.7), she comes to Jesus seeking
mercy for her daughter, and confessing Jesus to be both Lord and
Son of David. In spite of rebuffs from both the disciples and Jesus,
she persists with deep humility in her quest for her daughter's
healing. She refuses to let traditional boundaries exclude her from
grace. Her persistence is rewarded with the climactic pronounce-
ment of Jesus: '"O woman, great is your faith! Be it done for you as
you desire"' (15.28). What is important here is not only the fact
that Jesus acknowledges this Gentile woman's great faith, but also
that her faith contrasts markedly with the 'little faith' of the
disciples (cf. 14.30; 17.20).[15] What is more, her faith is on a par
with that of the Gentile centurion (8.5–13). Gentiles, both women
and men, belong by grace to the new people of God.

Fifth, and finally, women play crucial roles at the end of
Matthew's story, as at the beginning. At the Passion, there is
Pilate's wife (27.19). Like Joseph and the Magi in the Infancy
Narratives, she is the recipient of a revelation about Jesus in a
dream (cf. 1.20; 2.12, 13, 19). And like John the Baptist at Jesus'
baptism, she testifies to Jesus' righteousness (cf. 3.14–15). Just as
Jesus does not need to be baptized, neither does he deserve to die.
So the woman, another Gentile woman, is a witness to Jesus'
exemplary obedience.

Other women are witnesses too. In 27.55–6, we are told of the
'many women' followers of Jesus, including the two Marys and the
mother of James and John, who watch 'from afar' the stupendous
events accompanying Jesus' death (cf. vv. 51–4). So they witness
the beginning of the End; they (i.e. the two Marys) witness the
deposition of Jesus in the tomb; they witness the second earthquake
and the appearance of the angel who rolls away the stone; they
witness the empty tomb; they are the *first* to receive a revelation of
the risen Jesus; and they take their witness to the eleven.

4. Matthew's Gospel, then, is a story of women of faith as well
as men of faith. It is a story of the revelation of the grace of God in
the coming of God's Son to proclaim the kingdom of heaven and to
bring into being a community of 'mothers', 'brothers' and 'sisters'
(cf. 12.50) living in the light of the kingdom as children of the

heavenly Father. It is a demanding Gospel, though, for the revelation of grace brings with it the obligation to respond in obedience. This obligation, this paradoxically 'easy' yoke and 'light' burden (11.30), is placed upon all who would follow: at heart, it is not gender specific, just as it is not race specific. There *are* two ways, according to Matthew, but the division is not between male and female, but between the few who are 'wise' and the many who are 'foolish' (cf. 7.13–14, 24–7). Jesus *does* appoint men who are to be leaders of the faithful, Peter in particular (16.17–19), but nothing is said to indicate that their maleness is a necessary or sufficient qualification either for leadership or for succession to leadership. Faith and radical moral integrity are what is called for; and the model for leadership is neither a Mary nor a Peter, but the unique Son of God, who shows the way ahead and promises his presence (28.18–20).

III. THE WITNESS OF MARK

By comparison with Matthew, the theology of Mark is less anthropomorphic and the Gospel of Mark is less explicitly ecclesiological in its orientation. The picture of God as the loving heavenly Father who cares for his Son and for his children on earth as they are obedient to him in the life of the Church, is much more muted in Mark. Prominent instead is an emphasis on the hidden sovereignty and transcendence of God, the mystery of the divine purpose especially in relation to suffering, and the imperative of faith and watchfulness in the midst of darkness (cf. chs. 4, 13). As in Matthew, God is depicted as Father and Jesus as the Son (e.g. 1.11; 9.7; 13.32; 14.36; 15.39), while those who do God's will are identified as the spiritual family of Jesus (3.35). But the ethos of Mark is more sombre altogether. Mark has, as it were, stared tragedy more directly in the face without flinching. The Christian life, for Mark, is life on a knife-edge, life embroiled in chaos and contradiction, life and death endured even in the absence of God (15.34).[16]

1. This explains why, in Mark's story of Jesus, the events of the Passion bulk so large. Mark would have agreed fully with Paul, when he says:

Stephen C. Barton

> For Jews demand signs and Greeks seek wisdom, but we preach
> Christ crucified, a stumbling block to Jews and folly to Gentiles,
> but to those who are called, both Jews and Greeks, Christ is the
> power of God and the wisdom of God. For the foolishness of
> God is wiser than men, and the weakness of God is stronger
> than men. (1 Cor. 1.22–5)

Mark's Gospel is about the revelation of the mysterious love of
God in the suffering, death and resurrection of his Son, Jesus. The
death of Jesus is God's will (8.31; 9.31; 10.33–4), and Jesus
follows 'the way' to Jerusalem and death in obedience to God
(14.36). By the giving up of his life in death, he 'ransoms' many
(10.45): that is, he sets free from the domination of Satan (cf.
3.27) those who have faith in him and who show their faith by
becoming his followers on 'the way' (8.34–8).

2. This is a *subversive* gospel. It turns the world upside down.
As Jesus himself says: 'For whoever would save his life will lose it;
and whoever loses his life for my sake and the gospel's will save it'
(8.35). God is found, no longer in the Temple and the cult (15.38),
but through faith in his Son crucified and risen. The people of God
are defined, no longer in terms of the Law and the nation of the
Jews, but (again) by their faith in God's Son (15.39).[17] Sacred
space is located, no longer in Jerusalem or the Temple, but at the
cross and wherever the risen Christ 'goes before' (14.28; 16.7).[18]
Sacred time is determined, no longer by the religious calendar, but
by the coming of the kingdom of God and the beginning of the
End-time in Jesus' death and resurrection. Power lies, no longer in
the hands of Satan, nor of Rome, nor of the civil and religious
leaders of the Jews, nor with men, nor even with women (cf. 6.14–
29), but with the God who ransoms 'many' by the giving of his
Son.

3. I have said just now that the message of Mark is subversive
in a quite radical way. *No one is left in a privileged position.* This
includes women as well as men. Nevertheless, it is precisely
because salvation, power, and the pious life are the special preserve
of none, that they are open, now, to *all who have faith.* It is
conspicuous and noteworthy, especially given the deeply embedded
patriarchalism of Mark's day, that women in Mark exemplify this
revolution.[19]

First, there is the healing of Simon's mother-in-law (1.29–31). The grace of God in Jesus is not restricted to men. Jesus heals women as well (cf. 5.21–43); and this is the *first* of the healing miracles in Mark. The response of the healed woman is to 'serve' (*diakonein*) Jesus and the others. The language of service, here, is not necessarily menial. More likely it is Markan language for being a disciple after the example of the Son of Man (10.45; 15.41).

A second healing story is the striking account of the woman with a haemorrhage (5.24b–34). For Mark, this woman is a model of bold faith in Jesus, shown in action. The healing is unique in that it takes place solely at the woman's initiative. And, in response to Jesus' summons, she bears public witness to 'the whole truth' (v. 33), in contrast to the disciples who, typically, misunderstand. For so doing, Jesus acknowledges that her faith has 'saved' her and sends her on her way with the blessing of 'peace' (v. 34). Her story is an epitome of the Gospel as a whole. In a situation of chronic illness, ritual uncleanness (which will have excluded her from cultic worship), poverty and increasing hopelessness, she hears about Jesus, comes to him in faith and touches him, is healed (or 'saved'), and witnesses to the truth. Not only so. The skilful 'sandwiching'[20] of her story within the two halves of the story of the healing of Jairus' daughter (5.21–4a, 35–43), allows her to be a witness to Jairus (a ruler of the synagogue!) of the power of Jesus and of his need also for faith in Jesus (v. 36).

Another woman who shows bold, active faith is the Syrophoenician woman (7.24–30). Her story is as important for Mark as for Matthew. Crucially, it occurs between the two miraculous feedings (6.30–44; 8.1–10), the first of which is on Jewish soil and symbolizes the mission to Israel, and the second of which is in Gentile territory and symbolizes the mission to the Gentiles. Crucially also, it occurs immediately after Jesus teaches that the rules of *kashrut* (which separate Jew from Gentile as pure from defiled) are valid no longer (7.1–23). The coming of this Gentile woman to Jesus, her bold action in speaking up (with some persistence!), and Jesus' change of heart in response, express in a very powerful way Mark's conviction of a new order breaking in and the turning upside down of the old order. Barriers of race and gender hinder no longer access to salvation for people of faith.

Yet another exemplary person in Mark is the anonymous woman

who anoints Jesus' head (14.3–9).[21] The location of this story at the beginning of the passion narrative gives it great prominence. What the woman does expresses the gospel in a nutshell. In anointing the head of Jesus, she confesses symbolically her faith in Jesus as Messiah ('anointed one'). It is an action which contrasts vividly with the actions of leading men, descriptions of which frame this story. On the one side, the chief priests and scribes seek to kill him (14.1–2); and, on the other side, Judas, one of the twelve, goes to betray him (14.10–11). Her extravagant and costly gesture of self-giving love for the Jesus who is about to be crucified (v. 8), gains for her a response of approbation accorded to no other person in Mark's Gospel: 'And truly, I say to you, wherever the gospel is preached in the whole world, what she has done will be told in memory of her' (v. 9). This is striking, indeed. The memory of this woman's loving action[22] becomes itself an integral part of the gospel proclamation to the whole world. And this is fitting. For the woman functions as a Christ-figure, since the story of Jesus himself follows the same pattern: acts of self-denying service; experiences of conflict which lead to rejection and humiliation; and glorious vindication at the end.

We turn, finally, to the women at the end of Mark's story of Jesus. In a gospel which is full of surprises and reversals, one of the greatest surprises is the sudden mention of the 'many women' from Galilee who are there to witness the momentous event of the crucifixion (15.40–1), and the three women who are the only ones to witness the empty tomb and the angelophany (16.1–8). The significance of these women for Mark can hardly be overestimated. First, they are described in the terminology of discipleship: they 'followed' Jesus (cf. 1.18; 2.14) and 'ministered' to him (cf. 1.13; 1.31; 10.45). It is not only the twelve (men) who are disciples of Jesus: something which the other stories about women have shown us already. Second, from a cultural and religious viewpoint, they are relative outsiders who, by their (even limited) identification with the one who has been made an outsider on a cross, become insiders. In this they are like another outsider at the cross, the Gentile centurion, who comes to faith (15.39). Third, these women followers replace the men. The twelve have fled long since (14.50) and Peter has denied his allegiance to Jesus three times (14.66–72). Jesus' intimate circle, Peter, James and John (cf. 13.3; 14.33), is replaced by the three named women, Mary Magdalene, Mary the mother of James and Joses, and Salome. It is the women who become witnesses to these crucial events of salvation, not the twelve, as we would have expected. The effect is 'to compound the surprising reality of Jesus' crucifixion with the surprising reality of women's discipleship'.[23] Fourth, the three women are the first to hear the announcement of the resurrection, and it is they who are entrusted with the responsibility of telling 'the disciples and Peter' that the risen Jesus will appear to them in Galilee (16.7).[24]

4. In Mark's Gospel, then, as in Matthew's, discipleship of Jesus and bearing witness to the grace of God in Jesus are not privileges exclusive to any one gender or race or class. They are open, in a subversive and boundary-crossing way, to whoever puts his or her faith in Jesus. But faith is not just mental assent. As the stories of women show, faith means bold action and self-denying love for the gospel's sake. As the stories of women show also, such faith is likely to be found in the most unexpected places. Any suggestion that Mark, nevertheless, confines roles of *leadership* to men, beginning with the twelve (e.g. 3.13–19), fails to recognize, not only this evangelist's deep ambivalence towards the twelve,[25] but also his thorough-going critique of the conventional (and patriarchal) leadership patterns and power relations of his day (cf. 10.35–45, especially vv. 42–4).

IV. THE WITNESS OF LUKE–ACTS

The theology of Luke's two volumes is dominated by a 'salvation history' perspective according to which God's plan of salvation begins with Israel, is fulfilled in the coming of Jesus—his birth, life, death, resurrection, and ascension—and is being brought to fruition in the gathering of Gentiles as well as Jews into the people of God. There is a very strong emphasis on the *continuity* of God's grace, which binds closely together Israel, Jesus and the Church. There is also a very strong emphasis on the *inclusiveness* of God's grace, which extends the boundaries of the people of God, in a quite unprecedented way, to all who respond in faith to God-in-Christ and are baptized. Stories about women exemplify this theology, along with its implications for the life of faith.

1. For the evangelist Luke, as for all four evangelists, the coming

of Jesus and of his forerunner John signifies the dawning of the new age, the time of fulfilment, the time of eschatological salvation. Luke is so convinced of this that he writes his two-volume narrative to chronicle the amazing events which bear witness to the truth of what he believes (Luke 1.1–4). Most important for Luke in establishing his claim that God's new age has dawned, is evidence of *the powerful presence of God's Spirit* in fulfilment of scriptural prophecy. It is the Spirit who makes change possible by imparting divine power; and it is the Spirit who legitimates change by making God's will known.

So it is very noteworthy that, in both volumes, God's Spirit is present in a quite evident way, and that the Spirit works through women as well as men. John 'will be filled with the Holy Spirit, even from his mother's womb' (1.15), and Elizabeth herself pronounces a beatitude upon Mary by the power of the Spirit (1.41–2). The Spirit comes upon Mary to make possible the great miracle of the conception and birth of the Son of God (1.35) and to inspire her praise of God (1.46–55). Zechariah and Simeon prophesy under the Spirit's inspiration (1.67–79; 2.25–35), as does the venerable prophetess, Anna (2.36–8). John prophesies that Jesus will baptize the people 'with the Holy Spirit and with fire' (3.16); and this is fulfilled at Pentecost (Acts 1.5). Jesus himself has the Spirit come upon him in a most literal, and therefore undeniable, way, to empower him for his own prophetic work (3.21–2; cf. 4.1, 14, 18; etc.).

Luke's second volume might be more aptly titled, 'The Acts of the Holy Spirit'. The traditional title, 'The Acts of the Apostles', draws proper attention to the leading role accorded figures like Peter, John, Philip, James and Paul, but it diverts attention away from the crucial *theological and pneumatological foundation* of these men's work, and from the important roles played by a number of women who are not apostles (according to Luke). So, for example, Luke tells us that Mary the mother of Jesus, together with the women followers from Galilee, are part of the upper room company who are filled with the Holy Spirit and share in the powerful manifestations of the Spirit, on the Day of Pentecost (1.14; cf. 2.1ff.). The experience is interpreted by Peter in terms of a prophecy from Joel which is strongly inclusive in scope: 'And in the last days it shall be, God declares, that I will pour out my

Spirit upon all flesh, and your sons and your daughters shall prophesy . . . yea, and on my menservants and my maidservants in those days I will pour out my Spirit; and they shall prophesy' (2.17-18). We are not surprised, then, to find women as well as men participating in the new and charismatic common life which comes into being, and sharing its problems: 'And more than ever believers were added to the Lord, multitudes both of men and women' (5.14; cf. 4.32—5.11; 6.1ff.). Prominent amongst the women are Tabitha/Dorcas, a 'disciple . . . full of good works and acts of charity' (9.36-42); Mary, the mother of John Mark and the host of a Christian gathering (12.12-17); Lydia, a trader in purple goods, who becomes a Christian and serves as a benefactress to Paul and Silas (16.14-15, 40); Priscilla, who, along with her husband Aquila, become co-workers and fellow-travellers with Paul, and 'expound to Apollos more accurately the way of God' (ch. 18); and, in Acts 21.8-9, we are told that Philip had 'four unmarried daughters, who prophesied'.

All this is not to deny that Luke gives overwhelming attention to the twelve apostles (especially Peter) and to leaders in the mission to the Gentiles like Philip and Paul. I would not deny either that Luke actually *plays down* the importance of women in the life of the Early Church.[26] These considerations would be particularly important if we were trying to use Luke–Acts as a source for the historical reconstruction of the role of women in early Christianity. But, as I made clear at the beginning, reading the Gospels *as Scripture* is a different exercise. As Scripture, I would claim that Luke's two volumes are a strong and indispensable witness to the *divine reality* of the beginning of the new age of the eschatological Spirit, and that participation (*koinonia*) in the life of this new age is open, equally, to all. In Luke's day, it was important to emphasize that this meant the full inclusion of the Gentiles in the people of God. Today, we are much more aware that it is important to emphasize that it means the full inclusion and equal participation of women in the people of God, as well.

That Luke understands this too, in spite of the bias just discussed, finds support in the following considerations. First, Luke devotes more space to stories about women than do the other evangelists. Second, Luke's stories about women, especially in Luke 1—2, show the influence of biblical traditions about eminent women in the life of Israel (such as Sarah, Miriam, Deborah, Hannah, Ruth, Judith and Esther). Third, Luke's writing achieves a skilful and significant pairing of stories of men with stories of women: Zechariah/Mary (1.11–12, 27–9); Simeon/Anna (2.25, 36); the mother of a dead son/the father of a dead daughter (7.12; 8.41); the scribe/the two sisters (10.25–37, 38–42); the insistent man/the insistent widow (11.5–7; 18.1–8); the woman healed on the sabbath/the man healed on the sabbath (13.10–17; 14.1–6); the daughter of Abraham/the son of Abraham (13.16; 19.9); the parable of the shepherd/the parable of the woman (15.3–7, 8–10); and so on.[27] On the basis of evidence such as this, it is hard to deny that Luke's vision of Christian community is strongly inclusive, not only of Gentiles, but of women also.

2. The evangelist Luke not only wants to establish beyond any doubt that the new age of the eschatological Spirit, open to all people, has dawned: he wants also to convey *how to live* and *what qualities of character* are appropriate, in response to what God has done.[28] Important for us is the recognition that both women and men serve as models in this respect. We may take Peter's statement, in Acts 10.34–5, as a kind of bench-marker: '"Truly I perceive that God shows no partiality, but in every nation any one who fears him and does what is right is acceptable to him."' Of course, Peter is speaking of his profound discovery of God's acceptance of Gentiles, like Cornelius and his household, into the people of God. But what he says is applicable equally to other 'outsider' groups, including women.

Since Luke gives more prominence to Mary than any other evangelist, we begin with her.[29] Like any disciple, she is first and foremost a recipient of the divine grace, whose life is changed irreversibly as a result (1.28ff.). She is a person indwelt by God's Spirit (1.35). She is obedient to God's will, even though it involves what is impossible, humanly speaking (1.37–8). She bears witness to what God has done for her, as part of her witness to the gospel of God's grace for the poor (1.46–55). She is a person who does not get carried away by marvels, but gives herself to quiet introspection and remembering (2.19, 51). She is faithful and pious in her religious observance (2.21, 22ff., 39, 41ff.). She is a person whose commitment to God-in-Christ endures, in spite of testing (2.35), not being able fully to understand (2.48–50), having to accept the cost in terms of family ties (8.19–21; 11.27–8), and having to accept her son's humiliating death: for she is there, praying with the apostles, in Jerusalem at Pentecost (Acts 1.14). Mary, in short, is a true Israelite and a model disciple. The virtues and qualities she shows are the very qualities Luke wishes every Christian person to exhibit. They are the qualities shown by Jesus himself.

Elizabeth, likewise. With Zechariah, she is 'righteous before God, walking in all the commandments and ordinances of the Lord blameless' (1.6). Her obedience and piety are rewarded in an extraordinary manifestation of divine grace which removes her shame (1.7ff., 24–5). She too is Spirit-filled, and bears joyful, prophetic witness to what God is doing (1.41–5, 57ff.). It is surely no coincidence that the portraits of Mary and Elizabeth in Luke 1–2 are so rich in relation to what the evangelist wants to convey about Christian character. For their stories are bound up inextricably with the dawn of the new age in the births of John and Jesus; and the dawn of the new age is, at the same time, the time when the nature of Christian character is revealed.

Anna is another case in point (2.36–8). She is depicted as a person of truly biblical virtue: a woman of the Spirit (a prophetess); a woman of venerable age, and therefore wise; a woman of constancy (having remained a widow until the symbolically significant age of eighty-four); a woman of faithful devotion to God, shown in her lifestyle ('worshipping with fasting and prayer night and day'); and a woman who has remained open to the future and who bears public witness to the gracious work of God coming to pass. Again, like Mary and Elizabeth, a true Israelite and a model Christian disciple.

Finally, though by no means exhaustively, we may mention the woman who anoints Jesus (7.36–50). We saw how important this story is in Mark, where it comes at the beginning of the Passion narrative and expresses Mark's Gospel in a nutshell. The story is no less important for Luke, and functions in a similar way. But Luke has relocated it and modified it significantly. Here, it occurs shortly after the Sermon on the Plain, when Jesus pronounces God's blessing upon 'you that weep now' (6.21b), and teaches the multitude, 'Judge not, and you will not be judged; condemn not and you will not be condemned; forgive, and you will be forgiven'

(6.37f.). The woman comes to Jesus weeping (7.38) and finds blessing. She comes as a 'sinner' (7.37), and is neither judged by Jesus, nor condemned, but is forgiven. So the story of this woman in her encounter with Jesus expresses in a nutshell the salvation which God makes possible through Jesus, as taught by him in the Sermon. For Luke especially, Jesus is 'a friend of tax collectors and sinners': it is *they* who are children of the divine wisdom (7.34–5).

But it is very important for Luke to show that the grace of God is not cheap grace; and in this respect also the story of the woman has a paradigmatic quality. By her actions (for she speaks not a word), she shows true love and true repentance. Her tears are tears of penitence. Her anointing of Jesus' feet is an act of love and humility. Above all, in a Gospel where hospitality is a symbol of repentance and acceptance of the kingdom of God (cf. 19.1–10),[30] the kisses, the footwashing and the anointing by the woman, signify, in a way that words cannot, her acceptance of Jesus and the way of Jesus. So, like the penitent thief at the crucifixion (23.39–43), she finds salvation and 'peace' (7.50). Not only so, for, in a quite provocative way, her faith is contrasted explicitly with the obstinate unfaith of the Pharisee, Simon (7.39–47). In the words of the Magnificat (1.52), the mighty is put down and the person of low degree is exalted.

3. We may say, then, that for Luke, salvation works from the bottom up and from the margins in. *That* is the measure of God's grace. Acceptance of this radical and novel reversal of social-religious norms is difficult for those with vested interests in the status quo (cf. 14.15–24). In Luke's day, as in our own, such people are mainly men, along with the women who have been socialized into accepting men's ways. Change is possible only on the basis of a thorough-going repentance (*metanoia*; cf. 3.3, 8; 5.32; 15.7; 24.47; etc.). It is significant and noteworthy, that it is women who figure so often in Luke's two volumes both as active recipients of grace, and as models of the life of Christian faith lived in response to that grace.

V. THE WITNESS OF JOHN

Central to the message of the Fourth Gospel is the revelation of Jesus as the Word of God incarnate, the unique Son of God, who comes from the Father to reveal himself to the world as the true and only Way, and who returns to the Father to prepare a dwelling-place for those who believe in him. The underlying irony of the Gospel is that those who should have believed in him do not, and that those who seem unlikely recipients of revelation believe. The main aim of the Gospel is not just to elicit faith but also to confirm believers in their faith (John 20.30–1), as well as to provide a basis in the story of Jesus for believers to develop their own identity and life together as God's people. As we have come now to expect from the Gospels as a whole, the message of the Fourth Gospel is addressed to women as well as to men, and women play a very important part in the story which conveys that message.

1. 'In him was life' (1.4a). *That* is the fundamental claim of John, the truth to which his Gospel, and all the characters and episodes within it, bear witness. Where the other evangelists present Jesus primarily as the proclaimer of the in-breaking kingdom of God, John presents Jesus himself as the Life (14.6) and the one who gives 'eternal life' (3.16). This means that Jesus brings *a new order of creation* into being. Just as 'in the beginning . . . all things were made through him' (1.2–3), so now he comes into the world to reveal a new dispensation, the dispensation of 'eternal life'. The implications of this Christology and soteriology are immense.

Negatively, it means that the old dispensation has been displaced completely. The powerful use of path and residence metaphors (to use Margaret Davies' phrase)[31] throughout the Gospel, shows how strong is this sense of displacement. Now, Jesus exclusively is 'the way' to the Father, not Torah. Now, true worship takes place neither on Mount Gerizim nor on Mount Zion, but 'in spirit and in truth' (4.19ff.). Now, the only temple where God is to be encountered is the temple of Jesus' own body (2.21). In fact, virtually every major symbol of belonging as a Jew to the people of God—Torah, temple, festival calendar, sabbath observance, the land, the Scriptures, and the patriarchs—is displaced in a quite counter-cultural way by the Jesus of John.

Positively, the displacement of the old order of things means that the boundaries marking out the people of God have been redrawn and life as the people of God is practised in quite new ways. Now, in a radically universal way, salvation is open to all who believe in Jesus: women as well as men, and Greek and Samaritan as well as Jew. Now, the religion of the patriarchs (cf. 4.5–6; 8.31ff.) gives way to a religion directed by the Spirit (14.16–17, 26; 16.7–15). The life of faith is to be lived according to the utterly-demanding, 'new' commandment, 'love one another; even as I have loved you' (13.34). That is to say, the practice of the life of faith and the doing of God's will are open equally to women as well as to men in a way which the previous dispensation made impossible.

2. It is hardly surprising that 'eternal life', as offered by Jesus in his sign-miracles and revealed by Jesus in his discourses, provokes conflict and division amongst the people. The coming of a new order of things always generates resistance, especially if the identity of a people, its religion, its ways of ordering gender relations, and its ways of distinguishing insider from outsider, are put in question. In John, the division is felt very keenly indeed. It is expressed right at the beginning, in the Prologue (1.9–13):

> The true light that enlightens every one was coming into the world. He was in the world, and the world was made through him, yet the world knew him not. He came to his own home and his own people received him not. But to all who received him, who believed in his name, he gave power to become children of God; who were born, not of blood nor of the will of the flesh nor of man, but of God.

So people of the new dispensation are called 'children of God'; and this distinguishes them, as those whose Father is God and whose birth is a spiritual birth 'from above' (3.3ff.), from those who claim Abraham as their father (8.33ff.) and Moses as their guide (9.28–9). We are witnessing here a real parting of the ways. The mutual animosity is strong, too (cf. 16.1–4). But for the evangelist John, the painful separation is essential, and enormously liberating (8.31–2).

3. The stories about women express this liberating, counter-cultural faith very well.[32] The portrayal of the mother of Jesus is a case in point. As in Luke–Acts, she is presented in a positive light. Only this Gospel has the story of the wedding at Cana (2.1–11) and the episode at the foot of the cross (19.26–7). Strikingly, these two stories, in both of which Jesus' mother figures prominently,

frame the whole narrative of Jesus' ministry. They are also linked thematically. First, the 'hour' to which Jesus refers in 2.4, is the 'hour' of Jesus' glorification on the cross (12.23). Second, in both stories, Mary is never referred to by her personal name. Rather, she is accorded a representative status, being addressed by Jesus as 'Woman' (2.4; 19.26).

In the first story, replete as it is with resurrection and messianic symbolism—the 'third day', a wedding banquet, superb wine in abundance, the 'glory' of Jesus—the mother of Jesus is shown to be important, not by virtue of her natural tie with Jesus, but as a person who shows faith (however inadequate) in Jesus, and whose faith is deepened (2.4) and subsequently rewarded (2.5ff.). In the second story, she is paired with that other revered figure, the Beloved Disciple, at the foot of the cross as a witness of Jesus' 'hour'. Her presence there shows her faith in Jesus and that she has learnt the lesson of 2.4. It is this faith which is acknowledged by Jesus and rewarded: she is accepted into the family of disciples of Jesus as the 'mother' of the Beloved Disciple, who becomes her 'son'. Raymond Brown puts it well: 'If the Beloved Disciple was the ideal of discipleship, intimately involved with that disciple on an equal plane as part of Jesus' true family was a woman. A woman and a man stood at the foot of the cross as models for Jesus' "own", his true family of disciples.'[33]

We turn next to the story of the Samaritan woman (4.1–42). This story is not unrelated to the story of the wedding at Cana.[34] The messianic symbolism of new wine there is reinforced now by the metaphor of living water. The displacement of the cult symbolized there by the filling with wine of the six stone jars (*hudriai*) used for the rites of purification (2.6; cf. vv. 13–22) is reinforced now by the fact that the woman responds so positively to Jesus' words about true, spiritual worship (4.21ff.), and leaves her *hudria* behind (4.28) to go and tell her fellow citizens. And in both episodes, the story hinges on a conversation between Jesus and a woman who shows signs of active faith. By way of contrast, this Samaritan woman shows considerably more faith than Nicodemus, the 'teacher of Israel', in the immediately preceding episode (3.1–12)!

The story itself is remarkable. First, we note the pushing back of socio-religious boundaries by Jesus: he reveals saving knowledge to a Samaritan (4.9, 22), and that, a woman (of some notoriety, 4.17-18). The reaction of the returning male disciple tells all: 'They marvelled that he was talking with a woman' (4.27). Second, what Jesus offers the woman is of inestimable value: liberating knowledge about the nature of true worship and the coming of the Messiah. The first use of the revelatory *ego eimi* formula in John occurs here (4.21-6). Third, the woman becomes an evangelist and bears witness to Jesus, with the result that 'many of the Samaritans from that city believed in him because of the woman's testimony' (4.39). Her preaching achieves precisely what the preaching of the male disciples will achieve, according to 17.20. Not only so. For Jesus' words to the disciples, in 4.35-8 make explicit that her sowing of the seed has prepared the way for the apostolic harvest. In other words, she herself functions in an apostolic way.[35]

Mary Magdalene is another woman in John's story who functions in an apostolic way (20.1-2, 11-18). For Paul, according to 1 Cor. 9.1, an essential qualification for apostleship is to be able to say, 'I have seen the Lord' (*ton kurion heoraka*). It is precisely these words which Mary uses when she fulfils Jesus' commission and goes and announces the resurrection of Jesus to his (male) disciples: *heoraka ton kurion* (20.18)! The same words are used by the other disciples themselves when bearing witness to Thomas: *heorakamen ton kurion* (20.25). This is remarkable. It is as if the evangelist John is wanting to present Mary as quite on a par with the traditional apostles.

Other aspects of the account support this suggestion. First, John focuses uniquely on Mary Magdalene by omitting mention of the other women at the tomb of whom we know from the Synoptic traditions (e.g. Mark 16.1). Second, the story of Mary frames the story of the visit to the empty tomb by Peter and the Beloved Disciple (20.3-10). Her experience at least parallels theirs, therefore, and in one crucial aspect surpasses theirs: for she is the *first* to see both the angels (20.12-13) and the risen Jesus himself (20.14-18). Third, together with the Beloved Disciple, she displaces Peter. It is they who see and believe (20.8, 18), something which is not said of Peter, but which we are left to infer from 20.19-23. Whereas other early tradition claims for Peter the first resurrection appearance (1 Cor. 15.5; Luke 24.34), John claims this privilege for Mary Magdalene. Fourth, Jesus addresses her by name (20.16). For Mary, this is the delightful moment of recognition. She knows now that she is in the presence of the Good Shepherd who 'calls his own sheep by name and leads them out' (10.3). She is fully a member of the fold: as fully a member as the one whom Jesus calls by the name, Cephas, in 1.42. Finally, it is to Mary that the risen Jesus gives the crucial revelation about the nature of his resurrection life: that it is not a matter of mere resuscitation, but of ascension to the Father (20.17). Not without justification, then, has the tradition of the Western Church accorded this Mary the title, *apostola apostolorum*: 'apostle to the apostles'.[36]

The story of Mary, Martha and their brother Lazarus, in John 11, is another episode where a woman is given a role which other tradition gives to Peter. In Mark's Gospel, a climactic turning-point in the narrative is the confession at Caesarea Philippi by Peter: '"You are the Christ"' (Mark 8.29). This episode, so important for all three Synoptic evangelists, is completely remoulded in John (6.66–71); and the precise christological confession, '"You are the Christ . . ."' is placed, strikingly, on the lips of Martha (11.27). It is to Martha, furthermore, that Jesus first reveals himself as 'the resurrection and the life' (11.25).

This same story is very significant in other respects, too. We note that Mary and Martha, as well as Lazarus, are loved by Jesus (11.3, 5, 11, 33–6). Jesus *shows* his love for them by raising Lazarus from death: an act which costs him his own life (11.8, 45–53), and accords with his own subsequent teaching, 'Greater love has no man than this, that a man lay down his life for his friends' (15.13). But this love relationship is not just one-way, from Jesus to the family trio. It is a *reciprocal* love relationship. For Mary is introduced right at the outset as the one 'who anointed the Lord with ointment and wiped his feet with her hair': and this we are told, before the event has taken place (11.2; cf. 12.1–8)! This relationship of reciprocal love conveys the essence of what John means by 'eternal life': and it is shared between women and men alike. As the story of the anointing itself makes clear, such love is costly: it requires identifying with the one who is 'the resurrection and the life', in his death (cf. 11.7, 9–11). But it is also full of life-giving fragrance by which the stench of death and of the old order of things is overcome (12.3; cf. 11.39).

3. It is quite clear, therefore, that this evangelist goes further

than the others in giving equal prominence to female disciples as to male disciples, including the twelve. This is because, for John, discipleship is not about ecclesiastical authority of a patriarchal kind, as this is reflected in other parts of the New Testament (the Pastoral Epistles, in particular). John would have viewed this as a backward step into the old order of things, an intolerable compromise with 'the world'. Rather, discipleship is about belonging in love to the *spiritual* family of women and men who, as 'children of God', 'abide' in Jesus the Son and trust him as 'the way' to the Father.

VI. CONCLUSION

It is appropriate now to draw together some of the main findings of this particular theological reading of the gospel stories about women and Jesus. In so doing, I am very aware that there is a danger of being reductionist: of boiling everything down to a few morals in a way which does a disservice to the colour, imaginativeness, multi-dimensionality and open-endedness of the gospel stories themselves. But in an essay of this kind, the risk has to be taken. So, I offer the following conclusions.

First, all four Gospels are witnesses to the fundamental theological claim that the coming of Jesus inaugurates a new order of things: the kingdom of heaven (Matthew), the kingdom of God (Mark), the coming of the Spirit (Luke–Acts), eternal life (John). This new order is seen as an act of God's grace, a new covenant between God and humankind made possible by Jesus' life, death and resurrection, which brings into being a new community. The story of Jesus and the Samaritan woman in John captures this profoundly.

Second, the new community of the people of God expresses the grace of God by being radically inclusive. Gentiles are welcome, as well as Jews. Women are welcome, as well as men. A cameo of this truth is the story of the confrontation between Jesus and the Syrophoenician woman.

Third, acceptance into the people of God is accorded on the basis, not of race, nor of status, nor of gender, but of repentance and faith in Jesus expressed in a life of love. This is epitomized in the Lukan version of the story of the woman who anoints Jesus.

Fourth, the change of heart, breaking of stereotypes and redrawing of boundaries involved in becoming people of the new age generates resistance. It is a painful, costly, public business whose outcome is often far from certain. To save your life you have to lose it. That was true for Jesus. It was true also for the woman with the haemorrhage.

Fifth, the qualities required for leadership and positions of responsibility in the people of God are not gender specific. They are moral and religious qualities: gifts of God's sovereign Spirit, not accidents of birth. Hence the remarkable prominence and authority accorded women like the mother of Jesus, Mary and Martha, and Mary Magdalene, in the Gospel of John.

Finally, in so far as the gospel stories of women and Jesus are, for us, Scripture, they cannot be confined, safely, to the sphere of history. Rather, as we have seen again and again, they express the gospel in a nutshell. Therefore, they are to be proclaimed, and they are to be lived out in practice: '"And truly, I say to you, wherever the gospel is preached in the whole world, what she has done will be told in memory of her"'.

Notes

1. I wish to express my thanks to two of my Durham colleagues, Ann Loades and Walter Moberly, for their very helpful comments on an earlier draft of this essay; and to acknowledge the stimulus I have gained from working on feminist biblical hermeneutics with four postgraduate students in the theology department: Alison Simcock, Musa Dube, Sister Rosemary Howarth CHN and Katie Paul.
2. Jane Williams, 'Jesus the Jew and Women', in Monica Furlong, ed., *Feminine in the Church* (London, SPCK, 1984), p. 97.
3. J. L. Houlden, 'The Worth of Arguments', in H. Wilson, ed., *Women Priests? Yes — Now!* (Nutfield, Surrey, Denholm House Press, 1975), p. 19.
4. See the profound work of Robert Morgan and John Barton, *Biblical Interpretation* (Oxford, OUP, 1988).
5. See W. Klassen, 'Musonius Rufus, Jesus and Paul: Three First Century Feminists', in P. Richardson and J. C. Hurd, eds., *From Jesus to Paul* (Ontario, Wilfrid Laurier U.P., 1984), pp. 185–206.
6. The phrase comes from Elisabeth S. Fiorenza, *In Memory of Her* (London, SCM, 1983).
7. This point is made by Bernadette J. Brooten, 'Jewish Women's History

55

in the Roman Period: A Task for Christian Theology', in G. Nickelsburg and G. MacRae, eds., *Christians Among Jews and Gentiles* (Philadelphia, Fortress, 1986), pp. 22–30, esp. pp. 24–6.

8. See, e.g., the position of Daphne Hampson, in Daphne Hampson and Rosemary R. Ruether, 'Is there a place for Feminists in a Christian Church?' *New Blackfriars* (Jan. 1987), pp. 1–16.

9. I have found the following two evaluations of feminist theologies particularly helpful: Elizabeth Achtemeier, 'The Impossible Possibility. Evaluating the Feminist Approach to Bible and Theology', *Interpretation*, XLII (1988), pp. 45–57; and G. W. Stroup, 'Between Echo and Narcissus. The Role of the Bible in Feminist Theology', *Interpretation*, XLII (1988), pp. 19–32.

10. I am indebted here to conversations with Walter Moberly and, through him, to the writings of Brevard Childs. Very helpful also is the essay of Nicholas Lash, 'Performing the Scriptures', in his *Theology on the Way to Emmaus* (London, SCM, 1986), pp. 37–46.

11. See J. Z. Smith, 'Sacred Persistence: Towards a Rediscription of Canon', in W. S. Green, ed., *Aproaches to Ancient Judaism: Theory and Practice* (Missoula, Scholars Press, 1978), pp. 11–28.

12. The evidence is collected and surveyed in J. D. G. Dunn, *Christology in the Making* (London, SCM, 1980), pp. 13–22.

13. R. E. Brown, *The Birth of the Messiah* (London, Geoffrey Chapman, 1977), p. 74.

14. For two superb accounts, see W. A. Meeks, 'The Image of the Androgyne: Some Uses of a Symbol in Earliest Christianity', *History of Religions*, 13 (1974), pp. 165–208, esp. pp. 167–80, on 'Woman's Place'; and Ross S. Kraemer, 'Women in the Religions of the Greco-Roman World', *Religious Studies Review*, 9 (1983), pp. 127–39.

15. Interestingly, Eduard Schweizer sees this story as illustrating only 'the miracle of the faith of the gentiles'. He overlooks the fact that it is a Gentile *woman* who has faith. See his *The Good News According to Matthew* (London, SPCK, 1976), p. 330.

16. See further, J. L. Houlden, *Backward into Light. The Passion and Resurrection of Jesus according to Matthew and Mark* (London, SCM, 1987).

17. On faith in Mark, see C. D. Marshall, *Faith as a Theme in Mark's Narrative* (Cambridge, CUP, 1989).

18. See further the superb study of Elizabeth S. Malbon, *Narrative Space and Mythic Meaning in Mark* (San Francisco, Harper & Row, 1986).

19. In what follows, I have been helped especially by D. Rhoads and D. Michie, *Mark as Story* (Philadelphia, Fortress, 1982); Elizabeth S. Malbon, 'Fallible Followers: Women and Men in the Gospel of Mark', *SEMEIA*, 28 (1983), pp. 29–48; and A. Gill, 'Women Ministers in the Gospel of Mark', *Australian Biblical Review*, XXXV (1987), pp. 14–21.

20. On which, see further, B. van Iersel, *Reading Mark* (Edinburgh, T.&T. Clark, 1989), pp. 99–101.

21. For a more detailed study of this story, see my article, 'Mark as Narrative: The Story of the Anointing Woman (Mark 14.3-9)', forthcoming in the *Expository Times*.
22. In passing, it should be pointed out that her sacrificial action parallels in important ways that of *another woman* whom Jesus explicitly commends: the poor widow at the Temple treasury, who surrenders 'her whole living' (12.41-4). See the excellent analysis by Elizabeth S. Malbon in, 'Fallible Followers', pp. 37-9.
23. Elizabeth S. Malbon, 'Fallible Followers', p. 42.
24. The response of the women to the angelophany, in 16.8, is hardly one of disobedience, as is sometimes claimed. The whole presupposition of the Gospel is that they did tell what they had seen and heard! David Catchpole has shown, furthermore, that 'trembling', 'astonishment', 'fear' and silence are not responses of disobedience, but typical reactions to a revelation of the divine (cf. 4.41; 5.15; 5.33; 6.51; 9.6; etc). See D. C. Catchpole, 'The Fearful Silence of the Women at the Tomb', *Journal of Theology for Southern Africa*, 18 (1977), pp. 3-10.
25. On which, see J. B. Tyson, 'The Blindness of the Disciples in Mark', in C. Tuckett, ed., *The Messianic Secret* (London, SPCK, 1983), pp. 35-43.
26. See further, J. A. Grassi, *The Hidden Heroes of the Gospels: Female Counterparts of Jesus* (Collegeville, The Liturgical Press, 1979), pp. 85-91. Elisabeth S. Fiorenza draws particular attention to Luke's omission of a resurrection appearance to women, in contrast to Matthew and John, who both report that Mary Magdalene was the first to see the risen Christ! See her article, '"You are not to be called Father": Early Christian History in a Feminist Perspective', *Cross Currents*, 39 (1979), pp. 301-23, at p. 308.
27. See E. Schweizer, *The Good News according to Luke* (London, SPCK, 1984), pp. 142-3.
28. I am indebted here to the excellent study by B. E. Beck, *The Christian Character in the Gospel of Luke* (London, Epworth Press, 1989), esp. ch. 8.
29. See further, R. E. Brown *et al.*, *Mary in the New Testament* (Philadelphia, Fortress, 1978), ch. 6; and J. A. Fitzmyer, *Luke the Theologian. Aspects of his Teaching* (London, Geoffrey Chapman, 1989), ch. 3, on 'Mary in Lucan Salvation History'.
30. See J. Koenig, *New Testament Hospitality* (Philadelphia, Fortress, 1985), ch. 4; also, H. Moxnes, *The Economy of the Kingdom. Social Conflict and Economic Relations in Luke's Gospel* (Philadelphia, Fortress, 1988).
31. Margaret Davies, 'Path and Residence Metaphors in the Fourth Gospel', *Theology*, LXXXVIII (1985), pp. 118-25.
32. I am indebted here to R. E. Brown, *The Community of the Beloved Disciple* (London, Geoffrey Chapman, 1979), Appendix II: 'Roles of Women in the Fourth Gospel'; and J. A. Grassi, *Hidden Heroes*, ch. 4.
33. R. E. Brown, *Community of the Beloved Disciple*, p. 197. Cf. also the

discussion of R. F. Collins, in 'The Representative Figures of the Fourth Gospel — II', *Downside Review*, 94 (1976), pp. 118–32, at pp. 120–2.

34. See R. A. Culpepper, *The Anatomy of the Fourth Gospel* (Philadelphia, Fortress, 1983), pp. 192–3.
35. So, too, R. E. Brown, *Community of the Beloved Disciple*, pp. 188–9.
36. R. E. Brown, *Community of the Beloved Disciple*, p. 190 and n.336.

3 *The power of the Fathers*

Over the last seven years a central part of my experience as a
Christian minister has been the opportunity to share ministry in
my college with two women colleagues. It is impossible to
encapsulate the many dimensions of that experience in words. I
know that I have learnt much about myself, the pain of the
continuing barriers placed against women in the ordained ministry
in the Church of England, and the wealth of wisdom and insight
that will infuse and transform the priesthood in the decades to
come when women are ordained and given power and authority in
the Church. It would be tempting to portray the time solely in
bright colours but that would be a false picture and in many
respects is inappropriate to my feelings and forebodings about the
Church.

Indeed, it is the sombre hues and shadows that stick out at this
particularly critical juncture in our common life, fraught as it is
with the uncertainties and divisions of opinion. I have been on the
receiving end of anger about the obtuseness of an institution
which discriminates between women and men with regard to a
priestly ministry and about my inability to recognize the extent of
my power as a man. I have had to recognize the superficiality of
some of my identification with women manifested in my failure to
come to terms with the powerful position I have and the hurt that
is caused by the freedom that is mine to deny that power from
which women are at present excluded if I so wish. There have been
times when, liturgically, it has felt scandalous to continue to keep
the rules while sharing the altar with a woman priest. The
contradictions I experience within myself and the exclusiveness in
which I was engaged are moments of discomfort and perplexity.
There have been times when I have been completely at a loss as to
how to react when there have been few bearings for the course,
and past practice seemed to offer few guides.

I have also known dents to my pride. I like to think of myself as
a man who is learning to accept not apologize for those 'feminine'
parts of myself. I feel that I have glimpsed something of what Sara
Maitland calls 'the power of the Fathers' in the Church and in my

everyday life.[1] I have, however, learnt much about those deep-seated prejudices which inform my outlook as a man, however strong the 'feminine' characteristics. The experience of working professionally shows up the poverty of my vision and the extent to which I need to learn patterns of response, human relating and, perhaps above all, involvement in struggle, which have hitherto not been part of my experience.

That complex of experiences is linked to another. Over recent years I have learnt to value my feelings and to begin to understand something of the ambivalence of that world which formed me as a working-class boy in South Yorkshire and in the very different worlds of Cambridge and the Church of England. The understanding I have is frequently only tenuous and always difficult to articulate. But I am beginning to glimpse the chaos of feelings and desires which pervades and disrupts the order and discipline of how I am expected to be as a man, a theologian and a Christian. That chaos is untameable in that it can never be reduced to words or managed by explanations. That has left me frequently recognizing that I feel myself to be unclear, pulled in several directions at once, lacking confidence to express with coherence and clarity how things are for me and for the world in which I live. So to write of biblical interpretation in any kind of ordered way at this stage is also to acknowledge the importance of refusing to reduce, systematize and thereby satisfy those real or imagined professional expectations. I cannot bring myself to apologize for this, because the bewildering complexity of experience has led me to suspect neat solutions which seek to encapsulate the contradictory character of emotion and perception. My biblical reading is informed by a desire at present to remain within the Church and by a refusal to allow apparently recalcitrant and reactionary texts to determine our response. Yet to refuse to engage with them at all is in some sense to give up on the tradition and allow ourselves to submit to it. Our task is to struggle with it, even if we may have to admit that in the end it refuses to give us any blessing whatsoever.

It is a mark of our age that we have little confidence in ourselves and in our God's continuing capacity to surprise and to open our eyes. We look earnestly to the past for that golden age when everything was well. That is a dangerous illusion, for nostalgia is a distorting and dispiriting affection. Part of our malaise is in the way in which we use the Scriptures and the tradition. Too easily they are seen to be there to provide answers as if they were some self-contained manual for belief and practice. How far that is from a Christian understanding of a relationship with God which grounds our experience in the complexities of the here and now as much as the insights of our ancestors in faith. What was done in times past is surely there for our edification but is in no way prescriptive as we seek what the Spirit says to the Churches *today*. Our unwillingness to be open to that is evidence of our lack of trust in each other and in the God who calls us to move forward to that reign of peace and justice when we shall all equally be marked with God's name.

That part of me which would like exegetical tidiness yearns for the ability to offer a nicely rounded interpretative model. Experience tells me that I am a long way from having that within my grasp. There is much more listening to be done and ways of interpreting to be open to. I can echo something of what I have learnt from feminist interpretation. It has been part of a new way of reading the text of Scripture,[2] not solely among the exegetical elite of the seminaries and universities but at the grassroots. Like the theology of liberation with which it has so much in common its emphasis is on the method: starting where one is with one's experience (which for the majority in Latin America means an experience of poverty and for women an experience of oppression), understanding the reasons for that kind of existence and relating them to the story of the deliverance from oppression in the Bible and promoting action for change. This means that ordinary people have taken the Bible into their own hands and begun to read the Word of God not only in the circumstances of their existence but also in comparison with the stories of the people of God in other times and other places. In Latin America, for example, millions of men and women abandoned by government and Church have discovered an ally in the story of the people of God in the Scriptures.

This way of reflecting on Scripture is one in which story, experience and biblical reflection are intertwined with the community's life of sorrow and joy. It is a reading which is emphatically communitarian, in which reflection on the story of a people can indeed lead to an appreciation of the *'sensus ecclesiae'* and a movement towards liberative action. So revelation is very much a present phenomenon. The Bible is not just about past history only. It is also a mirror to be held up to reflect the story of today and lend it a new perspective. God speaks through life; but that word is one that is illuminated by the Bible: 'The principal objective of reading the Bible is not to interpret the Bible but to interpret life with the help of the Bible.'[3] So, where you are determines to a large extent what you read. This is a reading which does not pretend to be neutral, and questions whether any other reading can claim that either. It is committed to the struggle for justice, and the resonances that are found with the biblical story suggest that the quest for the so-called 'objective' reading may itself be unfaithful to the commitments and partiality which the Scriptures themselves demand. It may be critical of the text of Scripture itself, formed as it is within the struggles of a past age and formed by the particular concerns and place within the social formation of the writer(s). To be critical, however, does not mean the taking of the moral high ground with regard to the literary products of the past. Readings which arise out of contemporary struggles may cast light on those past struggles and compromises, so that our awareness of that ever present necessity to come to terms with the injustice of the present order of things may be illuminated by the light of the experience of the past.

The experiences of marginality, of oppression, of feeling second class and without a voice are at the heart of the dynamic which drives the whole Christian liberationist perspective in its various forms. The way in which Scripture has been read by women has opened up many perspectives lost to predominantly white male interpreters. That process of the recovery of women's voices in the Christian tradition and the insights yielded by the text when looked at from women's points of view can shake our complacency about the irredeemably patriarchal character of Scripture and the tradition of the Church. Yet it is important not to be too sanguine about it. The voices of women are marginal and almost lost. The tendency to drown them out is so great that sometimes there seems little point in seeking to redeem the irredeemable. Many women have felt that the struggle is futile and looked elsewhere for their resources. If ever I thought that I was wedded to a reading of the Christian tradition which viewed its patriarchalism as in some sense prescriptive and lacking resources for change, renewal and freedom from oppression, I would feel inclined to give up too. But at the moment I feel that an understanding of God and revelation demands that the present is taken seriously as a resource for our insight into God and that we are not tied to past formulations and experiences as our only way to God. Accordingly, we can take comfort from those marginal voices in the belief that the Spirit is never fully quenched even when nemesis apparently stares us in the face.

Of course, the Scriptures (as has ever been true) are a battleground for our struggles whether over responses to sexuality, the rights of women or political duties. In the case of the ordination of women, by resort to our favourite texts we can make an adequate (and in my view compelling) case for the extension of women's ministry to include the offices of presbyter and bishop. That argument, as with the opposing one, will be shot through with that complexity of assumption and particular interest characteristic of all our interpretation. To set out in an essay of this kind to offer a dispassionate account of the biblical evidence is not only hermeneutically short-sighted but particularly inappropriate. There is, it seems to me, a central dimension in our discussions. It is that complexity of emotional response to women entering what has been a hitherto male preserve and thereby inexorably, albeit subtly, transforming the patterns of centuries with their distinctive experience and presence. What I have written in the opening paragraph of this essay is indication enough that I cannot write as one who has not been shaped by my involvement. Surveys of the material are on offer which may offer more convincing cases than I have space to do here.[4] Reference to Deborah, Huldah, Priscilla and Phoebe is clear evidence of the rich strand of scriptural tradition pointing out that the service of God is not confined to men. Nevertheless the exclusive character of the service of tabernacle and temple and the dominance of men in positions of power in the New Testament witness are contrary indications. The mirror to myself as a man offered by some of the most problematic texts and the ambiguity of the biblical witness suggests a much deeper-rooted challenge, something of which I want to explore a little in this essay.

Much attention in the New Testament centres on 1 Cor. 14.34ff.:

As in all the congregations of God's people women should keep silent at the meeting. They have no permission to talk, but should keep their place as the law directs. If there is something they want to know, they can ask their husbands at home. It is shocking for a woman to talk at a meeting.

and 1 Tim. 2.9ff.:

Their role is to learn, listening quietly and with due submission. I do not permit women to teach or dictate to the men; they should keep quiet. For Adam was created first, and Eve afterwards; moreover it was not Adam who was deceived; it was the woman who yielding to deception, fell into sin. But salvation for the woman will be in the bearing of children, provided she continues in faith, love and holiness, with modesty. (Translations from REB)

Here in particular we appear to have that exclusive statement which backs up the lack of women among the twelve and the original apostles. 1 Cor. 14, with its uncertainty about its textual tradition (the crucial verses are displaced in some manuscripts and found at the end of the chapter), has led to the supposition that it is an insertion incompatible with what Paul says in 1 Cor. 11.5 ('but a woman brings shame on her head if she prays or prophesies bareheaded'). This seems unlikely, and in any case we do not solve the problem of the passage by suggesting that it was an interpolation. Unlike some others where the passage is omitted, for example the longer ending of Mark, this passage remains part of the text of the canonical Scriptures whether we like it or not. What do we do with it? Just ignore it and leave it to those who oppose women's ministry in the congregations to use it? Precisely what the issue was in Corinth we have no means of knowing. Yet Paul's advice is not entirely negative. It enjoins that they learn at home. Although the verb 'learn' is used infrequently in Paul's letters, it is not difficult to make connections with the usage elsewhere, particularly in the gospels. Learning in the context of Jewish education meant attention to the minute detail of tradition. Here Paul seems to contemplate learning taking place by women. One might argue that the spontaneous activities of the spirit contrast with others which demand a degree of knowledge of the tradition which had to be learnt. In this, the story of Mary and Martha offers a paradigm. Mary sits in the mode of student but in the unusual situation of being a *woman* student learning from the Master (Luke 10.39).

The other passage, 1 Tim. 2.14, is much more problematic. Its refusal to women of the right to teach or exercise authority seems to be unambiguous; its gross suggestion that salvation depends on bearing children seems so contrary to what we know of the gospel. It is demeaning to the breadth of women's experience and ruthlessly exclusive of those women who are childless. The justification for the silence of women is that they were deceived and so by implication are unfit to be leaders because they are 'the devil's gateway'.

Possibly this harsh statement may reflect a situation where women were exercising power. At least, once again as in 1 Cor. 14 there is no exclusion of women from the process of learning (2.11). Perhaps once being learned they could then be in a role to teach? But in accordance with the thrust of the Pastoral Epistles such eccentric activity is to be discouraged. Here we have documents which promote sobriety and good order. Christianity is depicted as a movement which needs to be as inoffensive and 'normal' as possible. Of course, in a situation where survival is important, social and doctrinal innovation is discouraged. Groups which are desperately seeking their own survival cannot afford the luxury of dissent or non-conformity. Hence the tradition is all important and pressures have to be resisted which seem to lead to the fragmentation of faith and practice. In fact, of course, most mainstream churches ignore the injunctions contained in these texts. Even when there is little formal involvement liturgically, as in the Roman Catholic Church, the extent of informal exercise of power in ministry and liturgy is enormous. In the Basic Ecclesial Communities of Latin America, for example, involvement of women is extensive with leadership roles everywhere apparent.

Passages like these in 1 Corinthians and 1 Timothy pose questions for me as an interpreter and as a man. Because I find the peremptory tone of 1 Timothy so insufferable, I cannot side with an institution that came out with such pronouncements consistently. My immediate negative reaction is an understandably apologetic response. But what is rejected so vehemently are strands of my own outlook which I prefer not to acknowledge. Perhaps there is something of the attitude of 1 Timothy in my approach to life which my lack of engagement with that text has enabled me to ignore?

If we seek to engage with the situation that might have confronted the writer of 1 Timothy, we might have an inkling of sympathy with that sense of realism and the need to survive and preserve the faith which may be expressed in the sentiments of these passages. I often have to recognize that I am not going to change the world immediately and so compromises with the old order are inevitable. There will always be tension between my cherished ideals and working out practical goals which can be achieved within the structures as they are. When the tension becomes unbearable do I admit that there is little point in staying in an institution which maintains injustice and so get out, or do I wait? If I choose the latter course then acceptance of the status quo may seem inevitable and resistance to immediate change the consequence. Of course, one may stay within an institution, bear some discomfort, refuse to compromise and constantly seek change. Nevertheless, the pressures to accept the status quo when you are an official can *feel* great indeed.

It is never easy to let go of the power which enables me to exist and survive and thereby risk losing what I have. For men truly to express their powerfulness as human beings informed by the love of Christ will mean them stepping down from official offices in the hope that women may take over those offices. That would be a very appropriate form of leadership to enable those less accustomed to such roles to develop their capacity and have the opportunity to explore patterns of leading and service. Such behaviour would not be out of line with the creation of space for ministry in the local congregations which Paul offered. There was no attempt by him to keep control because there was a vision of ministry which was both inclusive and not self-perpetuating.

There is another dimension to this. The Pastoral Epistles represent a good example of the application of an 'off the shelf' attitude to ministry. Parallels may be found to these offices in the practice of the contemporary synagogue. It is as if the crisis posed by the need to preserve and survive has led to the rapid use of other models. That is to some extent inevitable, but the problem comes if it hampers the process of exploration of other patterns of ministry which are going on elsewhere. In one area there is evidence to suggest that this may have been the case: the ministry of women and the prophetic ministry, both of which may have been linked. Many have pointed to the opportunities for women which the early Christian Church offered. There is much from early Christian literature which indicates its importance as an identifying feature of Christianity in the earliest phase of its existence. What it represents is the unpredictable face of divine service. No hard and fast rules for prophecy are ever possible. The prophetic spirit refuses conformity and predictability and of its nature abhors the false stability of the complacent. It is, therefore, open to criticism. It is a vocation which cannot be legislated for and which cannot be confined to men. It is no accident that the prophetic ministry fell into desuetude, possibly in part because of the openings it offered women. The involvement of women in the Montanist movement, for example, was a source of criticism for orthodox groups. Prophecy refuses to maintain boundaries and so cannot easily be managed or kept within the bounds of acceptability. Ordinary people might be inspired like Amos, and there is no restriction to family, status, sex or wealth. It is no wonder that it is the activity, notwithstanding the central role it plays in New Testament understandings of ministry, which find little concrete expression in church orders down the centuries. In the struggle for power its charismatic character makes it a poor forger of those alliances which guarantee the gaining of influence. The story of its marginalization and/or domestication is a large part of the story of the emergence of the Christian ordained ministry.

In a situation where women have been excluded from power and the formation of ministry for so long there will be few role models which are not imbued with a male vision. The process of articulating them may need an exclusively women's involvement and reflection. That is often hard for men to cope with: we do not like to be on the receiving end of that kind of exclusiveness. We may be tempted into thinking that we can offer women space, but that is to fall into the trap of supposing that it is our right to donate (though the reality of power relations means that this is what often happens). Within the fellowship of the Spirit there is a right to claim that space. This is exactly what two biblical stories suggest.

In Mark 5.21–43 the contact with the unclean, which had already started in the touching of the leper and the interaction with Legion, continues in the story of the raising of Jairus' daughter and the healing of the woman with a haemorrhage. By the time that Jesus reaches Jairus' house the young woman is dead and thus Jesus contracts uncleanness by his contact with her as he had with the leper (5.41). That continued overcoming of the taboos of society in the cause of the reign of God is found also in the healing of the woman with the haemorrhage, who for that very reason would have been in a state of perpetual uncleanness (Lev. 15.25). Jesus feels the power going out of him as the woman with the haemorrhage touches his garment. That decline of male power is something to expect and is an essential part of healing and the demonstration of God's reign.

In the anointing at Bethany (Mark 14.1–11) we note that Jesus is identified with an outsider, a leper, and the central figure of the story is a woman. She anoints Jesus and incurs the rebuke of others for the waste involved. What they could not recognize here was the significance of what was going on. Jesus the messiah was here and recognized as such by the woman, not in words but in deeds. The supposed waste was in fact a preparation for burial and not an extravagant act. It is difficult not to make the connection with other parts of the Bible here. In the Old Testament it is the priest who anoints (e.g. 1 Kings 1.39). A woman *claims* that right and is acknowledged by Jesus to have seen in the one destined to death the true pattern of messiahship (Mark 10.45), something that was to be recognized by the soldier at the foot of the cross (Mark 15.39). Jesus is reminding the witnesses of the event that what the woman was doing was very significant for him and that there would be opportunity enough when he was dead to feed the poor. Jesus is asking them to recognize that there was a terminus to his time on earth with them. That fact was being marked by the woman.[5]

In the exploration of models of God and ministry it is necessary for men not to demand of women too quickly what has taken centuries to develop. Women have been used to denying or suppressing their needs in favour of others. We should not overnight expect them to be able to articulate those longings, often too deep for words, merely to satisfy others.[6] Of course, we shall need to be open to what women say they want even if it makes us feel uncomfortable. The time is for waiting and watching and above all learning and being responsive to those who have begun to articulate and practise a distinctive pattern of ministry. As men we may too readily allow our needs to dictate what women might offer. It is easy to confine and stereotype the distinctive contribution of women to ordained ministry and subtly project our hopes and aspirations of what is lacking in ourselves on to women and, what is more, seek for the fulfilment of our deepest needs in our expectations of what women offer. There is no reason to suppose that the oedipal drama might not be played out in a variety of different forms in the relationships between women and men in ministry.

The ambiguity of the biblical material has been a subject of careful study by women exegetes. So, passages which seem to reflect the patriarchal concerns of another age and seem so resistant to other points of view yield interpretations which can surprise and challenge our assumptions. This is not, in the first instance at least, a matter of retrieving the biblical text from its patriarchal grip. The pervasiveness of this must not be diminished. Yet even the most conservative texts can be found to be shot through with a utopian strand which, however tentatively, challenges the dominant impression. The book of Revelation offers a good example of this. Its utopian drive will be readily acknowledged. Yet reservations must be expressed about the negative image of women here. The major problem concerns the portrayal of Babylon in chapter 17. The use of the imagery focuses on the woman's sexuality. It suggests that woman by virtue of her sexuality has led the nations astray. The picture is much more complicated, however. We need to bear in mind that the ultimate inspiration for the behaviour lies with the Beast supporting the woman. The city is described as an oppressor like the one of old (Babylon) oppressed the Jewish people and led them into exile attempting to destroy their culture and religion, as oppressive powers have done to subjugate peoples down the ages). Its wealth, gained by self-exploitation, is a mark of disorder. Prostitution is a symptom of a disordered world. It is a sign of the abuse and oppression suffered by women at the hands of economically more powerful men and an indication of what women have to do to ensure their survival and compete in a world where they have much less power. The reader is enabled to understand how the wealth of Babylon comes by ways other than those which God's justice requires in a world where God's shalom prevails.

Throughout the book of Revelation there is a negative strand in the portrayal of women: Jezebel, the new Jerusalem portrayed merely as an adjunct of the bridegroom whose life is governed by pleasing 'him', the exaltation of celibacy and the use of sexual imagery focusing on the woman as the transgressor. In some sense the vision of the new age seems to reaffirm all the old assumptions about women, backed up by the forceful actions of a God who sets out to conquer. Yet that is not the whole story. Amidst the thrusting imagery which seems so devoid of compassion and insensitive to the positive aspects of women's activity there are contrary strands which suggest something different. In chapter 12 the pregnant woman symbolizes the people of God. Indeed, the contrast between pursuit by the Devil and support by the earthly embodiment of evil in chapter 17 is a positive feature: woman is not wholly ambiguous and on the side of darkness, even if we have to accept that a passive role is accorded to the 'acceptable' feminine images. That is not without its positive side. Limited scope for Christian activity is a mark of Revelation. Violent revolutionary change is hardly a hallmark of Revelation's concept of witness. 'Endurance' is a dominant characteristic. In this both men and women are not mere spectators but their activity is limited to faith (12.9), readiness, the expression of their emotions (5.3ff.) and that perseverance through thick and thin which has always been a characteristic of women's roles in our disordered and oppressive world. But these roles are shown to be of ultimate importance and a significant contribution by their witness to the new age. They may seem pretty feeble in the face of the well organized mobility of the armies of the male-dominated imperium. The secret is that this is what really works, however unlikely it may appear at first sight. It is after all the lot of the Lamb with the marks of slaughter: lifeless and weak, it is the creature which brings God's salvation.

There is a similar point to be made about Romans 8. In that chapter there is a mixture of masculine imagery (divine sonship is stressed) alongside the use of the imagery of gestation and birth to identify the process whereby the new creation emerges. The imagery of divine sonship in this chapter is of equal importance. This passage together with Galatians 3 makes clear that sonship is a privilege of faith. In a male-dominated world where the right of sons to the patrimony is central (e.g. Gen. 27) the right to share in that privilege which belongs to the son who shares in the inheritance is something that women now have in Christ. Women now become heirs; they have the same status as sons. They enter into that world hitherto reserved for men. The use of the father/son imagery is essentially about the rights of those who share in the eschatological inheritance through faith in the messiah. In my view it has little to tell us about the intimacy of the believer's relationship with God. Its origin is the discourse about the messianic inheritance (2 Sam. 7.14) which, according to the original promise, offered that special status of sonship only to the king, the descendant of David. In the New Testament (and other Jewish works which speak of the divine 'sonship' as the destiny of God's people) it is about the sharing of the inheritance more widely than a royal line based on male succession. It is the inclusive right of women as well as men to share in the messianic inheritance and all that it involves.

The *waiting* for birth stresses something which our generation finds so difficult to cope with: God's reign comes not at our behest but with groaning, travail and after much waiting and patience. Our understanding of hope needs that perspective of toil and labour. The new age is not handed to us on a plate. The birth of a child is hard work. That labour is something that can only be dimly understood by those who have not gone through that process, and yet our ministry is impoverished unless we can understand a little of the stories of women who give birth and who with patience have been left to bring up children. That often means watching and waiting, those important characteristics of disciples as they wait for the new age with patience, longing and in the midst of many a struggle (Mark 13.33).

Too often male theologies have been preoccupied with God's transcendence. In the New Testament, in the midst of suffering and tribulation, there is a firmly centred hope for the world. That dimension of 'down to earthness' which is surely central to our

71

theology, rooted as it is in the Word become flesh, stresses the body and the tangible, refusing to allow primacy to the cerebral. Our minds and our souls are in no privileged position. We proclaim the resurrection of the body, the liberation of all that encompasses us and in which we are involved, not the flight of the ethereal bits of ourselves to an other-worldly God in an unearthly realm. This is a point made in the central chapter in Alice Walker's *The Color Purple*, which offers a graphic reminder of how often a male-centred theology can be disengaged from the experience of God whom Jesus tells us meets us in little people and the apparently trivial things of life:

> But what do it look like? I ast. Don't look like nothing, she say. It ain't a picture show. It ain't something you can look at apart from anything else, including yourself. I believe God is everything, say Shug. Everything that is or ever was or ever will be. And when you can feel that, and be happy to feel that, you've found It. . . . My first step from the old white man was trees. Then air. Then birds. Then other people. But one day when I was sitting quiet and feeling like a motherless child, which I was, it come to me: that feeling of being part of everything, not separate at all. I knew that if I cut a tree, my arm would bleed. And I laughed and I cried and I run all around the house. I knew just what it was. In fact, when it happen, you can't miss it. It sort of like you know what, she say grinning and rubbing high up on my thigh . . .[7]

We are left to speculate what might have been the contours of the presentation of Christian gospel and ministry if it had been by the hands of women. There is a yawning gap in the story of our human experience of God in Scripture and tradition. Attempts have been made to repair that[8] but the concerted insight of centuries is not going to be assembled overnight. We are afforded glimpses of what might be and the dimensions of our mission and ministry which leave much to be desired or lie in neglect. The male writers of the New Testament can be in touch with some of those ideas, indirectly or vicariously. Thus that aggressive side of Paul had to come to terms with the meekness and gentleness of Christ. The achieving purposeful apostle had to learn something of the office of waiting, endurance and even the groaning and travail which goes on in Christian ministry amidst the sadness and pain of the old order.

I could go on. For all the knocks to my pride and all the moments of bewilderment I feel privileged to be part of an exploration in the Spirit, every bit as positive, dangerous and without adequate maps to guide as the debates over the admission of Gentiles to the people of God. Perhaps it is presumptuous to make claims of this kind (and in so doing I realize that I implicitly make unfavourable assumptions about the position from which I dissent). Yet I feel there is something of the flavour of pain and uncertainty, insecurity and daring which characterized those tentative moves (many including some false moves, to be sure) which led to the Gentiles being recognized as fellow children of Abraham and Sarah on the basis of faith in Christ.

For this reason we are not at a moment when we can lay down hard and fast guide-lines about the use of Scripture, except that to indulge in old certainties or methods may not be the most appropriate way of carrying on our task. We need experiment, and that in two senses. We need the experiment which is attentive to that experience of women (and men) so that we may inject into our theology that wealth drawn from the depths of our emotions and our longings. It is a wellspring that will surely water the arid desert of exclusively cerebral preoccupations. Bringing together the stirrings of our heart and the discipline of our head in equal and fruitful partnership is long overdue in theology. Secondly, we shall expect that experience will involve us in experiment. The Spirit who reminds us of Jesus will engage us in the task of leading us into all truth and those greater works which Jesus predicted his disciples would share. We may find that our experiments may in fact coincide with the recollection of one who was not easily pinned down and whose activity consistently seemed to flout the bounds of convention.

According to Acts the council which discussed the issue of the conditions of membership of the people of God was offered distinctive contributions charting the role of experience (Peter's speech in 15.7ff.) and the argument enlightened by tradition (James' contribution in 15.13ff.). Those contributions were met with attention and silence (15.12). What they were discussing was indeed an awesome development, but as Peter indicates, 'God made no difference between them and us, for God purified their hearts by faith' (Acts 15.9). It is that experience of the living Holy Spirit in our midst, insistent and demanding, which requires that our reading of tradition is responsive to a new work of God. We may reflect that in the circumstances of the Jerusalem Council Jewish men decided the conditions on which pagan men and women could be members of the commonwealth of Israel. They were responsive to 'grassroots' pressure, yet had to exercise their power. In some ways it was a compromise which sits uneasily with the other parts of the story that the first Christians tell about their relationships one with another (e.g. 1 Cor. 8 and Rom. 14). It was, however, a tentative step forward rather than an attempt to draw back or even mark time. Today men in the Church, many holding positions of power at international, national and parish level, are faced with a similar challenge to that which confronted Jewish men in Jerusalem. As men we have power which we can choose to ignore or to exercise in ways which are responsive to the convictions of millions of women, that God's work among them requires recognition and action on our part.

I am grateful to Ros Hart, Bridget Rees, Catherine Rowland and Vicki Palmer for their helpful comments.

Notes

1. Sara Maitland, *Virgin Territory*. London 1984.
2. See the useful survey in the first part of E. Schüssler Fiorenza. *In Memory of Her* (London 1983).
3. C. Mesters, 'The Use of the Bible in Christian Communities of the Common People', in Norman Gottwald, *The Bible and Liberation*. Orbis Books, New York 1984. p. 122. and *Defenseless Flower*, CIIR. London 1989. Itumeleng Mosala's *Biblical Hermeneutics and Black Theology in South Africa* (Exeter 1989) is illuminating. For some suggestive comments see Letty Russell *Household of Freedom. Authority in Feminist Theology* (Philadelphia 1987).
4. For a concise summary in English see e.g. Mary Hayter *New Eve in Christ* (London 1987).
5. On these passages see e.g. *Believing Women*, experience-based Bible studies compiled by Ruth Musgrave (Women in Theology).
6. There are some salutary remarks on this theme in C. Olivier. *Jocasta's Children: The Imprint of the Mother*. Routledge. London 1989.
7. Since writing this I now note that this chapter forms a significant part of Daphne Hampson's post-Christian theology in *Theology and Feminism* (Oxford 1990).
8. E.g. R. Ruether. *Women of Spirit* (New York 1979).

4 *Is Christianity irredeemably sexist?*
A response to Daphne Hampson[1]

Daphne Hampson's book, *Theology and Feminism* (Oxford 1990), is a clearly expressed critique of Christianity from a feminist point of view. The aim of this short contribution is to set out some of what is central to her argument, and defend Christianity from her charge that it is irredeemably sexist. Much of Christian culture has been and is deeply sexist. There is no doubt about that. And it is something men must learn and repent of. But I want to maintain that Christianity need not be so; at its heart Christianity is gospel — good news — for both woman and man. So this article is an apologetic. But it is not offered argumentatively or triumphantly. Christian men have hurt Christian women, and for that I make no defence. Daphne Hampson's book is not simply an argument but is the statement of a position painfully arrived at. In criticizing her arguments I do not want to seem dismissive either of her or of the hurt of other women.

Since the Enlightenment, Daphne Hampson argues, there has been an ill fit between Christianity and modern thought (p. 2). It is intrinsic to Christianity that it proclaims a particular revelation in history. A cluster of unique events is vital to it. God revealed God's self in particular through them. Against this, Daphne Hampson states that she does not believe that the causal nexus of history or nature can be broken. As far as she is concerned, this rules out peculiar events like the resurrection of Jesus, miracles and uniqueness (p. 8). It follows from this, in her thinking, that the Christian story is false. Though purporting to tell us how God acted, it is a false history.

Then she takes a second step. This false history or story is a patriarchal history. 'The figure of Christ is that of a male figure, and that is not to be evaded' (p. 9). Indeed, Western religion has been a cause of actions which have deeply harmed women. The Christian Church has been a cause of sexism in the world. So historical Christianity stands condemned for being both untrue in its message and harmful in its social effects. As such, Daphne

75

Hampson argues, its story can no longer be taken as a medium which is transparent of God (p. 37). Various persons, recognizing the patriarchal past of the Christian story, have tried to reinterpret it. But Daphne Hampson rejects this. As an example she refers to Shakespeare's *Merchant of Venice*. If we read this and notice its anti-semitism, we may be bothered by it, and may even condemn Shakespeare for his anti-semitism. But we do not involve ourselves in re-reading it to make it more acceptable. We dissociate ourselves from Shakespeare's outlook (p. 40). It is the same with the Judaeo–Christian story of the action of God and human salvation. Why should we wrestle with this God, reinterpreting the Bible, and seeking a blessing from him, she asks? Why not just dismiss it?

So Daphne Hampson's critique of Christianity is in two stages. First, her not being a Christian has nothing to do with any feminist stance which she takes up (p. 41). She is not a Christian because she does not believe that nature and history could be other than closed causal nexuses. As a result, she cannot believe that Jesus is related to God in a way that is different from that of any other human being. Second, we are left with a Christian story, a myth, through which we try to find a religious identity and express how we relate to God. But why, Daphne Hampson asks, should we say of a myth that it is 'symbolically true' if it is a sexist myth (p. 43)? Why should we symbolize our deepest beliefs through a myth which jars with all that we believe to be moral (p. 43)? And then we have her own answer. If our goal is a religious situation in which women and men are accounted equals (p. 36), then we need to break with the past. The 'vehicle' of the Christian myth can carry us no longer. It is sexist to the core and the agent of much hurt. So let us create new myths and symbols which are adequate to this age and our fundamental moral beliefs (p. 44).

This is Daphne Hampson's basic argument. It is in the light of this that she turns to Christology. As she sees it, the problem of Christology for feminists is that 'Jesus was a male human being and that thus . . . as the Second Person of the Trinity, it would seem that 'God' becomes in some way "male"' (p. 51). This then gives the male human being a privilege. It is the most basic belief of Christianity, but it is fundamentally sexist and one sided. As far as women are concerned, 'how may they see in the Godhead an image of themselves?' (p. 51). Can there be a way of speaking of the uniqueness of Jesus which is not incompatible with the equality of women? Can Christ ever be an 'inclusive' symbol: one that includes women as well as men?

Once again, Daphne Hampson gives us a response at two levels. She, personally, does not believe the causal nexus of nature can be broken. So she does not believe that Jesus could have had a divine nature, or that he could have been raised from the dead. As far as she is concerned, Christianity is simply not true. But feminism raises the further question of whether these central beliefs of Christianity can even be ethical (p. 53). 'Is it not the case that a religion in which the Godhead is represented as male . . . necessarily acts as an ideology which is biased against half of humanity?' (p. 53).

So are the central beliefs of Christianity irredeemable and totally incompatible with feminism? Daphne Hampson reviews high Christologies, low Christologies and what she calls 'message' Christologies. All of them have their problems. Interestingly, it is Patristic Christology which she thinks seems to hold out most hope of being compatible with feminism. Patristic Christology revolves around an absolute conviction that Christ is one person from a union of divine and human natures, and a quandary as to how to express this. Attempts to express the nature of this union took different tendencies. There was a typically 'Alexandrian' approach, which tended to see the incarnation as a union of the eternal Word of God and 'human flesh'. It stressed the initiative of God the Word and minimized the human element. Its horror was that the incarnation should be seen as a merely external conjunction of two independent and previously existing persons. Were that the case, there would be no real union of the human and the divine; the incarnation would not be an *incarnation*, but merely the 'adoption' of an assumed man, who would work in association with God. In contrast, there was a typically 'Antiochene' approach, which tended to see the incarnation as a union between God the Word and a man. This was a maximizing of the independence and integrity of the human element. The horror of this approach was the idea that the incarnation should produce a confusion of the two natures, a fusion of the human and divine which lost the integrity of both natures. The instinct of the Patristic writers of both sides was that only God can save, and God can only save by a true union of God's self with human nature. The problem was how this was to be expressed. Should it involve a maximizing or a minimizing of the human nature?

Daphne Hampson does not involve herself with the detailed stances taken in this debate, but she quotes the principle of Gregory of Nazianzus, which both sides of the debate would have upheld: 'That which is not assumed is not redeemed' (p. 55). This is a statement of the fundamental belief that in the incarnation, God the Word assumed our human nature. As she rightly sees, what is important here is that God assumed our fallen humanity. There is never a question that only 'male humanity' was assumed. Here then, she concedes, is an expression of Christology which 'does not allow that differences of sex . . . are of significance Christologically' (p. 55). But although this model seems to offer hope, in that theologically, it is genuinely inclusive of both women and men, Daphne Hampson considers it ultimately flawed. In modern times we have lost the philosophical framework which allowed it to make sense to speak of God assuming human nature into God's self. And beside this, '. . . it is still the case that that human nature [which was assumed] was the human nature of a male human being' (p. 75). She concludes that, whichever way we look at it, 'the maleness of Christ is not to be evaded' (p. 75). That being her diagnosis, Daphne Hampson passes ethical judgement upon it. 'Christology gives a male human being a status which is given to no woman. . . . Such a religion as Christianity is a symbolic distortion of the relationships which I would have' (p. 76).

What follows from this? Daphne Hampson claims that 'Women are disrupted in their worship by the masculinity of [Christianity] to the point where it ceases to be for them a vehicle through which they can love God' (p. 85). Our whole inherited way of conceptualizing God, she argues, is largely the projection of a masculine way of understanding reality (p. 148). So we need to recreate the way in which we understand God into something which will be tenable in this day and age. But are there any building bricks left? Where are we to begin? Daphne Hampson has already argued against the possibility of uniqueness. So she does not believe that any particular revelation can become normative. Consequently, 'methodologically the place where theology arises must be out of our own experience of God . . . theology is predicated upon our perception of God, not on revelation . . .' (p. 150). Despite this, Daphne Hampson does not want to say that God is a human projection (p. 150). She wishes to retain the possibility of prayer, but warns us not to 'limit the possibility of prayer to a situation conceived as dialogue between an I and a thou' (p. 169). She is clear that for her the word 'God' 'refers' (pp. 150, 169, 170), though this is very unclear, as she suggests that it does not necessarily follow that 'the word refers to a kind of entity, one which could be distinguished from all else that is' (p. 170).

Has Daphne Hampson proved her case that Christianity is irredeemably stuck in a sexist past, and should now be jettisoned as both untrue and immoral? She presents a prophetic indictment against the sexism of Christian history and culture. That cannot be denied. But we must still ask if this is the heart of Christianity, if this is how Christianity must be, or if what Daphne Hampson has been attacking is bad theology and Christianity's false cultural expression which we must repent of, but from which we can grow away. There are three areas in particular where I would take issue with her presentation.

First, at the beginning of her discussion of Christology, Daphne Hampson speaks of the problems for feminists that Jesus was 'a male human being' (p. 51). She suggests that in consequence of this, western religious thought has been 'ideologically loaded against women' (p. 51). She asks whether a symbol which would appear *necessarily* male can be said to be inclusive of all humanity. 'Does it not give male human beings *privilege* within the religion?' (my italics, p. 51). This is a damning charge. What are we to make of it?

On a number of occasions Daphne Hampson tells us that she cannot believe that the causal nexus of nature can be broken. Because of this she rules out unique events as an impossibility. This commits her to a certain view of the world and whoever the God is whom this world implies. This is a God who cannot interact with creation. So what is that God's role? Surely that God is the transcendent clockmaker, who winds up the mechanism of the world, and then leaves it to its own inevitable processes? Every event in the world is necessary, and as such, can be traced back to a sufficient and necessary cause. And, to some extent, one could argue back down the causal chain to whoever or whatever it was that set the chain in motion. Now, let us apply this to the child born at Bethlehem. If you take the view that the causal chain cannot be broken, and that all events are necessary (we could make no sense at all of an uncaused event. It would simply not be part of the real world), then the baby *had* to be a boy, and one could indeed argue back necessarily to the kind of being who set the chain in motion, and accuse that being of sexism. It was a set up. If you look at the world through the eyes of Daphne Hampson then there is something very sinister in the birth of that boy baby. It was a predetermined event; the male was chosen, the female was rejected. The child was necessarily male and that is unavoidably sexist.

But we do not need to use these presuppositions. According to the Christian doctrine of creation, God did not *have* to create the world. It was not a necessary event. But God created out of grace. It follows that we cannot argue back necessarily and coercively from the world to God. God gave the world its own structures, which *need not* be the structures they are, and which thus do not contain their ultimate explanation within themselves. For instance, there are no necessary reasons why daffodils are golden not purple. That they are golden is not a *random* event (for it occurs within the structures of this world), but it is not a *necessary* event. It is a *contingent* event. How do we react appropriately to a contingent event? I suggest we simply accept it as gift. It simply does not make sense to suggest that there is injustice for purple things or privilege for gold things from the contingent fact that daffodils are golden. So, I suggest, it is with the birth of Jesus, a boy child.

What has gone wrong? By an old-fashioned understanding of natural law, under which miracle would be seen as interference (see John Polkinghorne: *Science and Providence* [1989], chapter 4), Daphne Hampson has abolished contingency and sees everything in terms of necessary events. This creates a plot scenario, hidden purposes and eternal inevitable decisions. I do not believe this is a fair accusation against Christianity. She is not letting the sexist cat out of the bag. It is more a case of putting a cat in a bag and then saying: Look, there is a cat in there.

Second, I would like to look more closely at Daphne Hampson's characterization of what is at stake in Christology. She begins with a figure of whom she can ask: How is he compatible with women? Or, What do he and women have in common? Though it makes sense to ask that question grammatically, I want to suggest that theologically this is certainly an extraordinary question, and probably a wrong one. So let us explore this. First, although she sees the strength and inclusiveness of Patristic Christology, with its affirmation that God truly united human nature to God's self, she finally rejects it, too, as sexist. Thus, 'Even if we take Patristic Christology, in which it is said that God in Christ took on humanity in which we all participate, it is still the case that that human nature was the human nature of *a male human being*' (my italics, p. 75). Now, that Christianity is essentially about the assumption or uniquely revealing role of *an assumed man* (*a male*) may be the message of some popular piety, or the teaching of modern liberal anti-Trinitarianism, but it has never been part of the carefully defined teaching of Christian orthodoxy. Here I would agree strongly with what Daphne Hampson says. If the exaltation of an assumed man were at the heart of Christianity, it would indeed be sexist to the core. But that is not the case, and what I believe she is attacking is another figure of straw. The Alexandrian tradition in Patristic theology constantly denounced any suggestion that the incarnation was the conjunction of God the Word and 'an assumed man'. The theology of this, that there was an independently existing assumed man, was condemned at the Councils of Ephesus and Chalcedon as the heresy of Nestorianism. The Alexandrians even jibbed at the definition of Chalcedon, considering it too divisive of the divine and human natures in Christ. In the following centuries they developed an even more subtle formula for expressing the divine–human union in Christ. The Greek word *hypostasis* means 'a personal reality', 'a personal being'. The later Alexandrians taught that the human nature assumed by God the Word in the incarnation was *anhypostatos* ('without its own *independent* personhood'—and if without person, then without sex) in itself, but in being assumed by the Word it was made *enhypostatos* ('personalized'). The incarnation was a creative and redemptive movement in which God the Word assumed human nature, bringing it into union and personhood at the same time.

What this says is that at the heart of Christianity there is God's creative redemption of *humanity*, not the assumption of a man.

But this can be taken further. Daphne Hampson refers to the Christological principle of Gregory of Nazianzus: 'That which has not been assumed is not healed' (p. 55). She is happy with this, as am I. It tells us that what God assumed in Christ was humanity, that differences of race, sex, hair or eye colour are not of significance christologically. So here, at the heart, Christology is inclusive. But let us not stop there. What do we mean when we affirm that God in Christ assumed our humanity? Did God in Christ assume just our bodies or our minds as well? Surely our minds as well, or, on Gregory's principle, there would be parts of us which would not be healed, as being unassumed. But if God in Christ assumed our mind as well as our body, then God lifted up into God's self all that is crooked and corrupt in our human nature. God lifted up our hate, our despair, our lust, our damaged human relationships, *even our sexism*. Gregory's principle is the affirmation that God so loved us that, even in our estrangement, there is no part of us which God did not make God's own.

What can we learn from this? I suggest we learn that we cannot split the question of *who Christ is* (Christology) from the question of *what he does* (soteriology). We can only understand who he is in the light of our understanding of his purpose. If we do split these two, who he is and what he does, then I suggest we end up asking questions which ultimately, in terms of Christian theology, do not make sense. It follows from this that Christ is not a figure whom we can meaningfully inspect from a distance and say: What have you to do with us? Because when we understand who he is, we understand that his *whole being and purpose* is to be on our side, to build a bridge to us, to enter and transform our deepest alienation. I suggest that Daphne Hampson takes the position of the observer, the onlooker. And just as our perception of other human persons is flattened through mere external observation, so she produces a flattened, two-dimensional picture of Christology.

Thirdly, I would like to consider Daphne Hampson's argument that the medium of Christianity, that the vehicle or symbol system, should now be jettisoned as hopelessly sexist, and that we should create new conceptualizations for God. Graphically, she asks: Why should we wrestle with this God, and seek a blessing from him, unless we believe that the text is from God? Why not dismiss it? Why should we say of a myth that it is 'symbolically true', if it is a sexist myth?

What does Daphne Hampson reject? A symbol system, a narrative or realm of discourse which is sexist. What does she want? A symbol system which is true to what it symbolizes (p. 44). Now the difficulty of this is that she is not allowing the symbol system actually to refer. Rather than allowing her attention to terminate on that to which the symbols refer, her thought terminates on the symbols themselves. Again, I shall suggest that this is the stance of the observer not of the participator. Let us borrow an example from Michael Polanyi. Let us suppose a student is being taught to use x-ray plates to detect the presence of cancer. Initially, she will only see the plates with various shadings, ghostly outlines and unrelated blotches on them. Initially, she will not know what the outlines are of, or what their meaning is. She will not understand how other persons see them as being full of significance. But gradually, as she becomes initiated into this world, as she becomes a participator rather than an observer, she finds that she no longer sees the outlines and blotches on the plates that she saw before. Now she has the skill and integration, an unspecifiable knowledge, to be able to 'disattend' from the 'symbols', and looking through rather than at them, can see what they represent. There is an interplay between the symbols from which she disattends and the realities she sees. As she becomes more skilled, she is able to see more and more detail on the plate, and as she disattends from it, so her diagnosis of the reality becomes more and more focused.

It seems that Daphne Hampson remains at the stage of looking at the outlines on the plate rather than looking through it. She seems to think that the symbolism *contains* the meaning. Indeed, she refers to Marshall McLuhan's dictum 'The medium is the message' (p. 108 and *New Blackfriars* [68], 1987, p. 9) which would imply that Christianity is inextricably tied to its sexist cultural context. But if she means this, then what she is saying is that the realm of discourse or symbol system does not refer at all. The symbolism is the reality. We do not look through and disattend from the symbols, for the symbols are all there are. But this is as if the student were to try to weave together a connected account of the blotches on the x-ray plate without ever taking account of what they referred to. Beyond question, the narrative of the Bible is sexist, and it has encouraged sexism in history and modern society which we must recognize and reject. But Christianity *is not* its narrative, nor is it encapsulated by it. And when we look at Christianity, our attention no more terminates on its narrative as an end in itself than the student radiographer's attention terminates on the x-ray plate as an end in itself.

And a final comment. Despairing of the sexism of the Christian 'vehicle', Daphne Hampson sketches an approach to a fresh conceptualization of God. '. . . methodologically, the place where theology arises must be out of our own experience of God' (p. 150). This is dangerous ground, and for all her honesty and self searching, I do not find it convincing. It is too reminiscent of figures like Hume, who were so sceptical of the external world that they would only admit to knowledge of their own immediate personal sense impressions. It is desperately difficult to engage in a process of reconceptualizing God with the scant equipment she permits herself. 'To affirm that the word "God" refers is . . . not necessarily to believe that the word refers to a kind of entity, one which could be distinguished from all else that is' (pp. 169–70). Does a reference to God include an identification of God? If it does not, and I refer to God a second time, can I be sure that I am referring to the same God? One can only meaningfully make a private reference if that private reference has *some* public criteria (if it is possible to get it wrong). Otherwise, one would never know that one had got it right. One can only meaningfully refer to God on the basis of one's private experience if one presupposes the grammar (rules of use) of the name 'God'.[2] And grammar is in the public domain. What I am saying is that I find it hard to see how Daphne Hampson's reconceptualizing of God on the basis of her own experience makes sense. To do theology, it seems that one needs a community.

Daphne Hampson offers us a lucidly written and searching critique of Christianity. She says much which must make us ashamed and more aware, but I do not think her case that Christianity is beyond redemption is proven.

Notes

1. I am most grateful to Peter Harvey, Thomas F. Torrance and Denise Newton for their comments on an earlier draft of this paper.
2. Cf. Wittgenstein, *Philosophical Investigations*, 257.

PHILIP SHELDRAKE SJ

5 *Spirituality and sexism*

I was brought up as a devout Roman Catholic and entered the
Jesuits, a clerical religious order, in 1964, aged eighteen.
Consequently, my early understanding of God and self was shaped
by the behaviour patterns and symbolism of traditional Catholicism
and later by Jesuit life. Inevitably, this continued to affect my
spirituality despite personal development and academic training.
The experience was partly life-giving yet also inculcated fears and
prejudices that I did not always recognize, let alone understand. In
particular, I unconsciously absorbed a patriarchal world-view and
sexist attitudes.

A PERSONAL STORY

I want to begin by telling something of my own story as the basis
for reflection because experience is the only authority which I can
claim. Such an approach has limitations for the story is mine alone
and other people may interpret similar experiences differently.
Equally, I admit that my description is based on hindsight, selective
and impressionistic, and reveals ambivalent feelings about my
upbringing. I hope that the result is not too detached. Finally, an
autobiographical framework may disappoint people who prefer a
more systematic approach to the issues. However, I wish to avoid
abstractions or colonizing other people's experience.

The Roman Catholic Church prior to the Second Vatican Council
was rich with symbolism and long-standing patterns of behaviour.
Catholicism was more than church-going or personal piety. It was
a self-contained culture that defined our identities and tended to
be rather inward looking. Our world centred upon the local church
in which the symbols of the sacred were particularly powerful.
This was a substantial Gothic building set in its own grounds. The
large west door was dominated by an unusually tall tower which,
to a small boy like me, was awesome in its strength as it climbed
heavenwards. The spacious interior had a sensual quality warmed
by gentle light from the tinted clerestory windows. Even now I
remember the characteristic smell of polish, incense, flowers and

candles. The liturgy, like the inexorable flow of a river, mesmerized me with its hypnotic murmurings and chant punctuated by organ and bells.

The church's sacred geography unambiguously proclaimed that *this*, rather than the world outside, was the house of God and the gate of heaven. Its focus was the sanctuary, enclosed by rails and grilles, whose size and decoration immediately caught my attention. At the far end was the altar, the heart of Catholic worship, dominated by a tabernacle in which the Blessed Sacrament was enclosed and pinpointed by a flickering light. As a child this was a powerful symbol of the mysterious otherness of God, veiled from human eyes. The beautiful Lady Chapel was a centre of devotional activity, particularly the mysterious world of women such as the 'Children of Mary'. In the aisles were the 'boxes', dark and private places where we queued for Saturday confessions. These initially held no fears for me but in my teens became a horrible trial as I struggled with the confusions of adolescent sexual awakenings and the anticipated reaction of the priest. Finally, there was the sacristy where clergy and servers prepared for the liturgy. While more accessible than the sanctuary it was still protected by various taboos. To gain right of entry, as an altar server, felt like an immense privilege and gave us an *esprit de corps*. It was the forecourt, as it were, of the sacred.

Catholics lived in the world but were not of it. Our culture was one of separation. Religious activities and separate schooling supported this as both ideal and necessity for we were different and, at the same time, had to be protected from a dangerous world. Our lives at home and school were marked by liturgical feasts, days of fasting and abstinence, seasonal devotions, daily Mass during Lent, family prayers and prayers in the classroom. My regular involvement at church and in the religious life of an all-boys school run by an order of brothers meant that men increasingly became my religious role models, and male religiosity came to predominate.

Spirituality touched our lives at every level yet did not typically *value* the everyday. There was a great sense of 'the holy', but tightly focused in sacred places, objects and times. 'Good Catholics' tended to be preoccupied with the dangers of sin, with discipline and faithfulness to community practices. 'Catholic guilt' has become something of a cliché but there is some truth in it. Religion was hierarchical with the spiritual plane above the natural and access to it mediated by a special class of people. Everyone knew their place, few questioned conventional roles, and important symbols of the sacred were carefully protected.

Our primary role models for holiness were priests and members of religious orders. They had 'vocations' and their life-style was carefully protected because dedicated to undiluted contact with the divine. Black robes, long prayers and an absence of any obvious sexuality set them apart as God's special friends. Women were normally excluded from the most sacred space, the sanctuary, while some lay *men* were allowed regular access. Even the 'good sisters' (as nuns were popularly called) visibly depended on male mediation for the sacraments. Although they had a special relationship with 'the holy', their absence from public aspects of church life reinforced a perception that women's religion was limited to private devotion and hidden service.

There were two childhood experiences which did not outweigh the predominance of church religion yet sowed the seeds of something more inclusive and personal. At home, my Anglican father chose, in religious matters, to keep largely in the background although in quiet ways he sought to remind me of a wider world and broader sympathies. My mother's strong personality and firm Catholicism were more overt influences. On one level, she was very traditional and communicated an unquestioning respect for the Church, clergy and traditional roles. Yet, precisely because religion was so central to her life, my mother's way of parenting, combined with her personal spirituality, imaged a God and ways of responding to the divine that were different in many respects from public religion. Devotion to Mary was important for her but this was less an 'idolatrous' *substitution* for God than an implicit recognition that she desired contact with another face of *God*.

The second experience counter-balanced the tendency of church religion to enclose the infinite in precise symbols and rituals. Children often have an unselfconscious mysticism associated with an intense sense of place and harmony with nature. Sadly, many people later lose touch with this because it is overtaken by a more rational, 'adult' religion and Christian fears of pantheism. The result can be a 'Father Sky' versus 'Mother Earth' dichotomy. My own intense sense of place was associated with the depths, power and broad horizons of the sea near my home. The seascape was infinitely varied, reshaped by the ever-changing effects of light, wind, sky and tides. The sea also has many voices — the deep roar of breakers or the whisper of water on shingle. It demanded no explanation for it spoke directly to the heart, not the intellect, of an immense reality enfolding me and in which I could simply be. There was awe but no fear. From an early age I learned to be at home in the water, to let go and be supported by it, to become somehow part of it. It was an experience of the infinite which was, at the same time, to be face to face with the inner mystery of myself. For me, the sea was and is neither particularly masculine nor feminine but personal in a way that moves beyond gender stereotypes. When I left home I lost touch with the sea, with place, and this separation accentuated, I now realize, a sense of disconnection in my experience of God and self.

I entered a religious order on leaving school. Recently, I read about a survey among British Army officers' wives which suggested that many military men were ignorant and afraid of women and uncomfortable with sexuality because their youthful backgrounds had been dominated by 'boys, men and dogs'! With some obvious qualifications, most people who entered Religious Life over twenty years ago had similar limitations. We came from devout Catholic families, had received a single-sex education and entered an all-male world at an early age. I do not believe that celibacy in itself necessarily breeds misogynists any more than marriage automatically produces non-sexist attitudes and equal relationships. But male celibacy became a *culture* that dominated the Church and made sexist attitudes unavoidable.

Sexism was not necessarily blatant but women were viewed with suspicion or treated with patronizing paternalism. When I entered Religious Life its male variant had certain unhealthy features. It was a world where close contacts with lay people, especially women, were rare. The framework for thinking, speaking and relating was clerical. Our identity, loyalties and relationships were largely defined by community. The pervading spirituality demanded a surrender of our wills at an age when most of us had not yet reached a secure sense of identity. Spirituality was also ascetical, characterized by an emotional distance from God and other people. The affective dimension was not strongly encouraged and was even viewed with apprehension. Virginity was still seen as a higher way and sexuality was, at best, a background inconvenience cloaked by a physically and mentally demanding schedule. The prevailing atmosphere tended to heighten more unattractive aspects of male culture. Communities were short on affirmation and long on criticism and judgement. Individuals were easily stereotyped and this, combined with occasional verbal aggression, tended to undermine self-confidence and make self-disclosure and vulnerability even harder.

IMAGES OF GOD

This brief description of my story raises a central question for reflection: Where do I believe God is to be found? The answer has profound implications for our valuing of experience and under-standing of 'the self'. This in turn determines whether we believe that everyone naturally encounters the sacred or that privileged access belongs to an élite. One of the most radical challenges to traditional spirituality has been the realization that conventional images of God led many Christians into a flight from nature and from themselves, into concentrating spiritual resources in a few hands, and to a belief in the God-given superiority of men over women.

The concern for inclusive language witnesses to the power of words to evoke feelings and shape experience. However, I want to concentrate on a broader Catholic 'language of the sacred'. A strongly sacramental religion imaged an intimate God, especially in the *feeding* of frequent Communion, although this was hedged about with qualifications concerning worthiness. God was loving, yet the main emphasis was on God's mercy tempering the divine inclination to impart justice. Hence the need for so many advocates, Mary and the saints. Overemphasis on liturgical ritual tended to obscure the sacramental nature of all things and imaged a God absent from the specifics of people's lives. Paradise where God lived was our real home. This world was a 'vale of tears' rather than a 'vale of soul-making'. The word 'paradise' derives from the Old Persian for a walled garden. The sanctuary and its ritual was indeed a garden enclosed. Ritual reflected the spiritual hierarchy

Philip Sheldrake

of the 'court of heaven' which in turn reinforced an established social order. Christ was an ambiguous figure. There was the agonized man on the cross and the open arms of the Sacred Heart. Yet, the humanity of Jesus tended to be underplayed and with it the radical implication of incarnation that human nature and the world image the divine. I undoubtedly connected Jesus' maleness in a literal way with the nature of God but the significance of the historical particularity of Jesus was already distorted by *prior* assumptions about God and the superiority of maleness.

This male God was closely associated with two ideas, *power* and *distance*. The God of the sanctuary, separated by grilles, was an Olympian, possessed of immense power. This God required righteousness yet seemed to find all our efforts wanting. It was, if you like, Luther's classic dilemma! God also appeared to be at the top of a hierarchical pyramid above the clergy; the final authority in a world of rules and spiritual bureaucracy. God judged the world but, more immediately, was judge of our petty lives, faithful to unchanging laws imposed 'from above'. God's special magic could, however, be unleashed in our favour especially through guaranteed channels and authorized persons.

IMAGES OF SELF

The image of a distant and unchanging God, coupled with a dilution of Jesus' humanity, affected my conceptions of selfhood. There seemed to be a fixed cosmic order, reflected in human life especially in the Church, which meant that stable social roles and stereotyped action outweighed the value of individual personal lives. This reinforced a spirituality of duty—not only to fulfil one's proper role in life but to 'come to be' as a person.

Social concepts of masculinity harmonized pretty well with this God. It was possible to identify God in a special way with my maleness. This inevitably produced tensions because this maleness was flawed in that it forced me to repress aspects of myself and led to imbalances in my relationships. My eventual realization that such conceptions seriously limited my own identity was a vital first step towards rejecting exclusively masculine images for God, even modified ones, as destructive of everyone's identity.

When I was twelve my father died and I was told to be 'the man

90

of the house' and to be strong—in other words, according to the typically English definition of a 'real man', free-standing, autonomous, and controlled. The consequence for most men was a high valuation of objectivity and cool judgement. Emotion evidenced a lack of control. Images of God as self-possessed, invulnerable and perfect tended to reinforce this. It was difficult to accept vulnerability and incompleteness and easy to be guiltily preoccupied with lack of perfection and sin. To become an 'adult' male, you freed yourself from natural weaknesses, gained certain desirable powers, and took up specific roles. The greatest anxiety was about loss of self-possession. This was especially threatened by sexuality and the vulnerability inherent in intimacy with people and God.

Three important consequences for spirituality follow from the dominance of a flawed masculinity. Firstly, feelings, passion and natural impulses are feared. This had its effect on approaches to prayer, especially a suspicion of mysticism and emotion. The asceticism of seeking a healthy balance between the various dimensions of the human personality easily overbalances into a suspicion of materiality and a neurotic rejection of the body. In male-defined spiritualities, at least, sexuality (in practice, reduced to genitality) became a negative preoccupation.[1] The entertainment of sensual delight risked the unbridling of the demon lust. Only by abjuring fleshly pleasures could the spirit be liberated.

Secondly, the need for self-possession led to a fear of absorption and of 'the void'. Undoubtedly this had physical roots but the male sexual preoccupation with penetration and domination also relates to fears about men's relationship with God, especially inwardness, passivity, letting go and being enfolded—even about death.[2] Finally, the model of personhood which values power and control tends to produce a concern for good performance, organizational achievement and coherence. In personal spirituality this relates, for example, to a preference for structured prayer, a tendency to give prominence to the powers of reason and to fear intuition or feelings. Collectively, the Church may come to suspect the unconventional, the mystical, the prophetic, and the wildness of the Spirit. This relates closely to the dominance of a perfection model of spirituality. The 'archetype' of perfection rarely connected with individual experience and so was oppressive. It was also associated with an emphasis on power.

IMAGES OF WOMEN

Because assumptions about maleness were in reality the norm for *human* identity and behaviour they were the yard-stick by which women were measured. In effect, to become a 'spiritual' person demanded a rejection of 'raw nature'. But women were identified as closer to nature, partly, I suspect, because of male fears about women's mysterious bodily cycles which so emphasized their sexuality. A disembodied spirituality, with a high view of spiritual purity, necessarily had problems not only with sexuality but with women as such. Both can easily be seen as snares or pollutants. Hence misogyny. Women were more easily seduced and were themselves determined seducers.[3] For St Bernard, every woman was a threat to chastity. 'To be always with a woman and not to have intercourse with her is more difficult than to raise the dead.' Abbot Conrad of Marchtal is reputed to have said that 'the wickedness of women is greater than all other wickedness of the world, and that there is no anger like that of women, and that the poison of asps and dragons is more curable and less dangerous to men than the familiarity of women'.[4] *The Spiritual Exercises* of St Ignatius Loyola, prominent in Catholic retreats and parish missions, is by no means the most overtly sexist spiritual text. Yet, there is one strikingly misogynist image in the Rules for Discernment:

> The enemy [the evil spirit] conducts himself as a woman. He is a weakling before a show of strength, and a tyrant if he has his will. It is characteristic of a woman in a quarrel with a man to lose courage and to take to flight if the man shows that he is determined and fearless. However, if the man loses courage and begins to flee, the anger, vindictiveness, and rage of the woman surge up and know no bounds. (Exx 325)

Ascetical spirituality atoned for men's failures but was a reparation for women's very identity. Here, the spirituality of self-surrender took on a particularly powerful meaning. The regulations in the ninth-century *Regula monachorum* concerning the enclosure of nuns spoke of natural vanity being stripped away in the 'tomb' of the convent.[5] Because women were under the sway of instinctual processes they were deficient in reasonableness. It would seem natural, therefore, for men to exercise authority because presumably they alone could be authoritative. The fourteenth-century theologian Jean Gerson said that women were forbidden to write and to teach because 'All women's teaching . . . is to be held suspect unless it has been diligently examined, and much more fully than men's', for 'it is not proved that they are witnesses of divine grace'.[6] Any attempt by women to move beyond the limits set down by men threatened the very fabric of society and Church because their over-emotional and chaotic nature made them incompetent to handle their own lives, let alone other people's.

The Church has frequently been ambivalent about the religion of women. The logic of sexism is that women need spirituality more than men to control their nature yet women's devotions and mystical inspiration, as non-institutional avenues to God and sources of authority, were feared. This was associated, I suspect, with an unacknowledged fear of women's life-bearing identity which appeared to give them a natural *power* which men could not control. It is a short distance from these fears to the notorious witch-hunts of the sixteenth and seventeenth centuries.

CONVERSION AND LOSS

The challenge to a male-dominated spirituality and Church involves more than a greater sensitivity to language or equal participation by women in Church life and ministry. What is asked of men is a profound conversion in ways of thinking and being and this is inevitably difficult and painful.

It is especially hard in a celibate culture. I have had recent conversations with two other men, one a fellow-Jesuit, concerning the negative behaviour towards women of some priests and male Religious. Things have improved in recent years. Blatantly misogynist humour and sexual innuendo are less frequent. Religious houses are more open, individual priests and Religious have women friends and others are accustomed to collaborative work. Yet, we concluded, it is difficult to escape from a kind of low-key, yet pervasive sexism when together with other celibate men. The single-sex education of many may be a factor—at the very least the majority of celibate men did not get to know women as equals, friends or work-partners at the most impressionable

93

periods of their lives. Priests are not really taught how to be *receivers* — not least in interpersonal exchanges. For many, women are still 'the unknown' and ignorance leads to a fear that women cannot really be trusted because they think so differently, are unpredictable and difficult to reason with. Some celibate men still talk of women as manipulative and desiring control. Marriage is often viewed as a loss of freedom and celibacy as a protection of freedom. The *culture* of male celibacy can too easily become like the male club, the army mess and the masonic lodge — a safe environment where men can 'be themselves' without fear of women's presence and interference.

Even today, sexuality is rarely discussed among male celibates. There is sometimes a lack of integration and a tendency to associate feeling-denial with effective ministry. This is not helped by fears of 'losing a vocation' if men try to break out of this pattern. I also suspect that a private macho culture among celibate clergy is partly a reaction against the fear of being seen as sexless or effeminate. A 'group profile' of Catholic priests in some ten British dioceses about five years ago indicated a more general malaise. Some 40% viewed human nature as basically negative, and only 27% saw openness to experience, trust in others or affirmation of others as central values. Measurement of ego-development, the ability to make adequate responses to the complexities of life, was not encouraging. Only 14% scored as autonomous or integrated and some 55% as conformist. If accurate, this profile suggests that the destructive side of 'celibate culture' will perpetuate itself unless radical changes take place.[7]

Conversion always involves repentance, but it is often easier to admit to personal sexist peccadillos than to the structural sin of patriarchy in which I and other men share through the continued security we derive from it. To repent of this would imply a radical change of structures, roles and ways of relating and will not simply make us better people while leaving us in the same social or ecclesial position as always. Conversion at this level entails an experience of real and profound loss which will touch the very roots of how men have chosen to identify and value themselves.

I believe that to let go in this way demands a freedom that comes only from a personal, not merely theoretical, realization that there really are more fruitful ways of being and acting. To recognize the destructive elements in our lives is an important first step but insufficient on its own. Classical spirituality gave the impression that 'detachment' from negative forces was a stage prior to the freedom to respond to God's promptings. However, in practice, I believe that it is the very experience of being attracted to something better that leads gradually to a realization that we have already begun to move away from what binds us. Specifically, patriarchy ceases to be a theoretical issue and profound change starts to take place only when we begin to listen not only to the voices of women but to our own inner voices which speak to us of our damaged selves, the flawed nature of our relationships, and yet of the possibility of a new freedom.

Clearly revisions of our images of God will be inevitable and vital. The Christian tradition, despite its historical limitations, has always affirmed that God is beyond our control. A striking image is that of Peter's vision before visiting the centurion Cornelius in the Book of Acts, chapter 10, in which God challenges some of his inherited beliefs about where God is to be found and how God acts. We affirm the power of the Spirit to blow where God wills and lead us into all truth, however much Christians throughout history have been uncomfortable with this disruptive side of God and the unpredictability of this kind of leading. We need new interpretative paradigms as functions of liberation, but we also need a profoundly contemplative openness because there we meet an ever new and challenging face of God which ultimately has the greatest power to alter our perceptions.

We need to recover a greater balance between imaging God and recognizing that the ultimate reality of God is necessarily beyond images. To seek God through images prevents us from losing touch with God's movement towards us in and through creation, our human experience, and in incarnation. Created reality is not a distraction from which God is utterly removed. However, the Christian tradition also speaks of a journey beyond images. We cannot ultimately *reduce* God to human categories, let alone to male-centred ones. God will receive many names and yet always remains beyond every name. Indeed, the potential 'infinity' of images for God finally draws us into the mysterious depths of God beyond naming and the limitations of human reason. Difficult though it may be, imaging and denial are to be held in paradoxical tension.

Although the question of women's ministry is part of a more

complex tapestry, my changing reactions to this are a useful litmus test of broader adjustments. After ordination I inevitably ministered *to* women and indeed felt that I had learned a great deal from many of them. Later, the opening up of Jesuit work to greater collaboration with others meant that I worked and ministered *alongside* women. This taught me more about women's ministry and spirituality and was a better, if painful, education in the realities of equal and reciprocal relationships than any abstract discussion of the issues. There came a point, however, when my search for a more holistic spirituality and a developing consciousness about women made me realize that I needed to be *ministered to* by women. This led me to break with the Jesuit tradition of seeking retreats or spiritual direction exclusively from fellow-members and thus, by definition, from men.

Despite these experiences, I have to admit that it is not easy to listen to women's pain and even anger at their treatment by men in the Church. It is sometimes difficult to defend my choice of ordained ministry in a patriarchal Church and to affirm my belief that Christianity can change radically. On the other hand, it is easy to retreat into self-justification, or behind the reassuring walls of an all-male community because, at some level, I still share a male fear of loss of identity. With something as deeply-rooted as patriarchy and sexist assumptions, conversion may indeed be a life-long process.

CONCLUSION

Most of our working images of God have been one-sidedly influenced by traditional Christian fears of pantheism—a belief that God can be identified with the created universe. So, God easily becomes *totally* 'other', separated from ourselves and from creation. This grounds all the other separations we tend to impose—between material and spiritual, men and women. Yet, the Spirit, the underestimated person of the Christian Trinity, is God *indwelling* in all creation, all people; the *within* of all things. That reality of God, as the depth of all, invites us beyond our artificial separations and stereotypes to a realization of our inherent harmony with earth, with woman, with man.

To end on a personal note, I have found concrete images of God increasingly unsustaining even if the loss of them has been painful and even confusing. At times, my spiritual experience has been a struggle to stay with imagelessness, dryness and a sense of emptiness. I am gradually beginning to recognize in this experience a kind of liberation—from stereotyping God and other people but also, perhaps, from classical male fears of loss of control. It may even be that this loss was necessary in order to provoke other changes. However, one image from the *Showings* of Julian of Norwich has spoken particularly to me. Funnily enough, it is not the feminine imagery for God, although that too is moving. In Chapter 10 of the Long Text there is Julian's consoling vision of the bottom of the sea, with its green hills and valleys, seaweed and gravel. Julian understands that she is as safe in the sea as anywhere because God is there. I discovered Julian's image at much the same time as I understood my need to return to the sea, not merely physically but spiritually too, there to find a grounding of self in something which speaks to the heart and on which it is impossible to impose definition or limit.[8]

Notes

1. Caroline Walker Bynum, in *Holy feast and holy fast: the religious significance of food to medieval women* (Berkeley/London. 1987). argues that sexual abstinence was predominantly a male ascetical preoccupation.
2. It was recently suggested to me that visionary literature is predominantly female and the literature of imagelessness predominantly male. If true, it may well be that the latter kind of mystical experience represents a liberation from typical male fears of negation, passivity and absorption.
3. A comment of the fourteenth-century theologian, Jean Gerson, quoted in Caroline Walker Bynum, *Jesus as Mother: studies in the spirituality of the High Middle Ages* (Berkeley 1982), pp. 135-6.
4. The two quotations appear in R W Southern, *Western society and the Church in the Middle Ages* (London 1970), pp. 314-15.
5. Cited in Jane Tibbets Schulenburg, 'Strict active enclosure and its effects on the female monastic experience (500-1100)', in John Nichols & Lillian Thomas Shank, eds., *Distant echoes*, Medieval religious Women, vol 1 (Kalamazoo 1984), p. 60.
6. See n. 3.
7. These statistics are quoted in Gerard Burke, 'The contemporary priest:

Philip Sheldrake

experience and identity', in *The Way Supplement*, 56 (Summer 1986), pp. 124–36.

8. I am very grateful to the following people with whom I discussed this essay: Sophie Ball, Michael Barnes, Lavinia Byrne, Sylvia Carter, Ron Darwen, Kathy Donnelly, Suzanne Fageol, Frances Teresa, David Lonsdale, Anne Murphy, Dorothy Nicholson, Thomas Plastow and Catherine Ryan.

JAMES P. MACKEY

6 *The use and abuse of Mary in Roman Catholicism*

'The use and abuse of Roman Catholic doctrines about Mary and of devotion to her, and more particularly the ways in which such use and abuse affects the status of women and the roles they are allowed to play.' That is how the title of this chapter would read, if titles were allowed to be longer. Indeed the title might need to be longer still, to add some such phrase as: 'in the Church and in society at large'. For I would not like to convey the impression, if only by default of an added phrase, that Roman Catholic Marian doctrine and devotion affect the roles and status of women only in the Roman Catholic Church, or even in church circles ideologically close to Roman Catholicism, such as the Eastern Orthodox and the High Anglican. It is a commonplace of social philosophy, at least since Marx, that religious ideas, images and rituals, form an important part of the ideology by which all the people in any society secure to their satisfaction the validity of their main social structures and most conventional social processes. And I fully accept the force of that contention. People do use religious beliefs to prop up power and its unequal distribution in human societies, and they will always do so.

I do realize, of course, that this commonplace of social philosophy has been used as an argument for the modern reduction of religion to the point of its non-existence. Reductionist arguments are always of the 'religion is nothing other than' type. In the case of social philosophy reductionism suggests that there are powers which function in human society through particular people or groups; these powers deeply affect the prospects of life or death for most of us; and religion, which always images for us the arbiter of life and death, is 'nothing other than' these social powers personified as divine beings rather than being recognized in their human embodiments. I can only pause here in these introductory paragraphs to suggest that the truth of the matter is quite the opposite to that put forward in these reductionist arguments. We are indeed conscious of power in society on which our individual lives, their diminishment or enhancement, depend. These then prove to be amongst our main indicators when we seek to envisage the greater power over life and death in the world that is shared by all our societies. Social forms, as well as natural or cosmic categories, provide our images of the divine, and these images in turn shape our attitudes to society, as well as to nature and cosmos. Think of the ecological theologies that presently pullulate. Hence the attempt to think through the power structures of any society, on the one hand, and the religious quest, on the other, are most intimately related, and do mutually condition each other. The reductionist argument simply reads this phenomenon in the one single direction, boiling religion down to social power structures rather than seeking in social manifestations of power clues to its ultimate nature and origin. In support of my contention of the inadequacy of this uni-directional reading of a rich and complex phenomenon, I can only offer here the verifiable suggestion that even the most secular of societies regularly appeal to absolutes having all the binding power that gives religion its name. In social terms there are neither atheisms nor agnosticisms, there are only idolatries, shot through very occasionally with realized visions of the true God.

It is, however, neither this general argument about religious ideologies and society, nor the direction in which it is most cogently aimed, that is of most immediate interest to me here. It forms a necessary background, but the immediate interest is its illustration in Roman Catholic Marian doctrine and devotion. It is in any case a simple fact that people, all peoples, so persistently use religious symbolism (or its secular substitutes) in order to secure social forms. I want to take the example of Marian ideas, images and devotions, particularly in my own Roman Catholic tradition. I want to know how this Marian material was used, and how it worked. More particularly, I want to know if its use has been to the detriment of women and, if so, how it might be used to their advantage. That is my project; but in this short piece I can only outline the analytic part of it, and guess at some possible practical results.

In order to share in the securing of social forms in the manner indicated above, Mary would have had to share in the distinctive qualities of divinity. Did she ever do so? I have no doubt that in

popular piety, particularly in countries like Italy, Poland and
Ireland, where there are powerful traditions of devotion to Mary,
she did, and still does.[1] Since the Holy Spirit frequently enjoys no
more than a very ghostly presence in popular piety, the 'real'
Trinity revealed by the prayerful experience of the people consists
of the Father, the Mother, and the Son.[2] Of course, if anyone were
to ask any of these 'simple' faithful a question as crude as: Is Mary
God? the answer would almost certainly be an 'orthodox' negative.
But that would reflect less of the real state of affairs than of the
relative success of indoctrination by authorities. What, then, is the
status of Mary in the public theology and doctrine of the Roman
Catholic Church? Always flirting with the divinity of Mary, I
should be inclined to answer, but always finally, officially and
loudly denying it. A rather tortuous, and slightly devious process,
all things considered, but one which illustrates in its own way the
relevance of this Marian theology to the social status of women in
the Roman Catholic Church and the societies in which the ethos of
that Church predominates. Some examples, then, of this public
theology and doctrine.

Take first the oldest Marian doctrine, defined at the Council of
Ephesus in 431 CE, the *Theotokos*, Mary as God-bearer. That
council conferred that title on Mary because a prominent theologian
of the time, one Nestorius, was taken to imply that Christ was
really two—an eternal son of God somehow united in the flesh
with a very human son of Mary, two sons, with Mary the bearer
only of the human one. To call Mary *Theotokos*, God-bearer, it
was felt, would point up the real unity of the Christ, for it implied
that Mary bore the Son-of-God-incarnate, or, to make the matter
more articulate, that Mary's bearing of the Son of God was the
incarnating of him. She was then, in this sense, God-bearer. The
point of interest to us, however, is this: the title, God-bearer,
having satisfied the need of this anti-Nestorian strategy, then
begins to take on a life of its own, a life in which it gradually seems
to suggest a share in divine status for Mary herself. Some historians
of doctrine believe that this begins to happen when *Theotokos*,
God-bearer, begins to be translated by, or replaced by, the more
significant term, mother of God. These say that, whereas God-
bearer can be restricted to reference to the singular act or event of
incarnation, mother of God connotes a much more general

relationship of persons and so could elide the distinctions between the human and the divine. I accept that there is some such difference between the terms, but in the case of divine beings it is suggestions of their genesis that can be dangerous, long before discussion of broader or restricted meanings of different words for genesis comes into play, and God-bearer already conveys suggestions of genesis. So I believe it was particular ways of explaining the term, mother of God, rather than the term itself, which gradually, surreptitiously, but perhaps not altogether unintentionally, came to suggest some share in divine status for Mary. Here is an example of what I mean.

At times Mary's motherhood of God is severely qualified. The seminal Council of Chalcedon in 451 CE, for example, made it quite clear that the Son of God, as to his divinity, was born of the Father, and of the Father alone, in eternity, and that it was 'as to his humanity' that he was born of Mary 'in recent times'. Such qualification makes it quite clear that a fully-fledged divine person was generated and existed for an eternity before Mary's role began, and it correspondingly restricts the amount of meaning that can be read into Mary's motherhood of God. Other formulations, however, seem either ignorant of or impatient with such stringent qualification. Anxious to stress that Mary 'really', 'truly' is the Mother of God, these make such points as the present pope makes, namely, that 'motherhood concerns the whole person'.[3] Now if we were to take such reasoning at face value, the theological tradition would leave us in no doubt that the 'whole person' in question here is the divine Son, second person of the blessed Trinity. Chalcedon's qualification would disappear, and the old principle established so effectively against the Arians, that generator and generated must be 'of one and the same substance or being' would create in our minds pervasive impressions of the divinity of Mary; just as at the more popular level insistence that Mary is 'truly', 'really' God's Mother would be heard loudly and clearly over the more nuanced qualifications designed to remove any suggestion of Mary's own divinity as a result of her giving birth to Jesus of Nazareth. Popes who write like that are either innocent of required theological sophistication in these matters, or deliberately conveying impressions of Mary's divinity which in other contexts they will carefully deny, as we must shortly see them do.

A recent liberation theologian from Latin America also comments on the conception of Christ by Mary, the event which gave rise to the title of God-bearer, as described particularly in Luke's Gospel; but he goes very much further towards ascribing divine status to Mary as a result of this event than any pope has ever gone. He actually writes of a 'hypostatic union' between a divine person and the human Mary, the very term used in the tradition to define that union between the divine Son and the humanity of Jesus which makes Jesus divine. Using traditional trinitarian theology, he suggests that the Holy Spirit must have creaturely embodiment as part of its 'sending' into the world, much, one must suppose, as the Son had creaturely embodiment in the flesh of Jesus of Nazareth. But where Augustine, for example, would have seen such embodiment of Spirit in fire or the form of a dove, our theologian suggests the Spirit forges a kind of union with Mary parallel to, and causally connected with that which the Son or Word formed with the flesh of Jesus. His final proof text is Luke 1.35, which talks of the Holy Spirit coming on Mary and *therefore* 'the fruit to be born of Mary will rightly be called God'. Blithely ignoring the fact that 'son of God' and its equivalents can be used in the Bible without any suggestion of properly divine status, he informs his readers that this *therefore* in Luke 'establishes a causal nexus between the divinization of Mary and the divinization of the fruit conceived in her womb. Mary is assumed by the Holy Spirit, and thus elevated to the level of God.'[4] Boff goes so far as to suggest that the habit of the 'simple' faithful of putting Mary where the Spirit might be expected is then an example of *perichoresis*, an ancient theological technique for involving each of the three divine persons in the creative and salvific works of the others, lest any invidious differences of an Arian hue open up between them.[5] Used in this context, it can only mean that the simple faithful have two divine persons (at least), the Spirit and Mary, that they frequently honour or postulate the latter when we would expect the former, but that Boff has provided the theological justification for what they, in their simplicity, unwittingly do.

It is obvious enough, perhaps, that a Latin American theologian who has become interested in the oppression of women as much as in the oppression of the poor in general, should be even more anxious than a pope to elevate the feminine to a point as close as possible to divinity. His stated principle is: 'The divinizer of the masculine (with the feminine) is the Word. The divinizer of the feminine (with the masculine) is the Holy Spirit.'[6] But the distancing move is made again, for Boff describes all of this as a mere *theologoumenon*, that is to say, a kind of theological green paper, not the expression of his mature conviction as a theologian that this is or ought to be the official doctrine of the Church. And yet, although Boff and his fellow liberation theologians have been censured for much of their main-line theologizing, he has not, to the best of my knowledge, been taken to task over this Mariological *theologoumenon*. The sense of ecclesiastical ambivalence surrounding this matter increases the more one thinks about it.

Take next the figure of the divine woman, *Sophia* or Wisdom, who appears in such books as the Book of Proverbs (8.22ff.), the Wisdom of Jesus Ben Sirach (24.3), and the Book of Wisdom (7.21ff.). She is there described as God's first-born or first-created, God's image, and as creator, sustainer and pervader of all things, pitching her tent in Israel, and so on. *Sophia*, we are told, together with cognate titles like *Logos* or Word and *Pneuma* or Spirit, is a symbol, indeed in her case, a personification of God's own creative, providential and salvific power. At least from the ninth century in the West[7] the imagery connected with this divine woman in the so-called Wisdom literature is applied to Mary, particularly in the Marian Office, with which the great Alcuin was somehow connected.[8] Now it is well known that the earliest 'high' Christology, the earliest extant Christology which proposes what later came to be called more abstractly the divinity of Jesus, was cast precisely in imagery borrowed from that same divine woman in just these passages from Wisdom literature: Jesus as first-born (coming from the mouth of God as) word or breath, image of God, by whom all things were fashioned. One needs only to read such Pauline material as 1 Corinthians 1.18–31, Colossians 1.15–20 (in addition to the opening to the Fourth Gospel, to Hebrews, and texts like Revelation 3.14) to see how clearly this is so. One is then, of course, left with the question: how can the application of this imagery so successfully secure the conviction of the divinity of Jesus, if it does not secure some similar conviction of the divinity of Mary? The very least that can be said at this point is that the same sense of ambivalence begins to emerge here, as in the case of different treatments of the image of Mary as Mother of God.

People use a distinctive creation imagery in order to profess their faith in the divinity of Jesus, and naturally leave one wondering if they intend the same result from the use of the same imagery for Mary.

Take, finally, the matter of Mary's role in the redemption of the race. Here once again the language used is often redolent of divine status, but here, in clear contradistinction to the other two types of discourse we have been examining, impressions of divine status for Mary are constantly and explicitly rejected, so that any possible ambivalence in the matter is quickly removed. Before asking why such clarity about Mary's creaturely status, and in particular about her total subservience to Jesus, seems so necessary in the context of soteriology, look briefly at some examples of traditional talk about Mary's role in redemption. Hilda Graef in her *Mary: A History of Devotion and Doctrine* traces to the East, and in particular to one Germanus of Constantinople (d.733 CE), the origins of strong language about Mary's role in our redemption. This language came to the West, she believes, through one Ambrose Autpert (d.784 CE), an abbot who was in contact with Greek immigrants in Sicily. The language reaches a certain peak, and crystallizes in the title 'co-redemptrix' in the last century of the last millennium, in the works of one who bore the winsome name of John the Geometer.[9] Stated in very general terms, the role now attributed to Mary in redeeming the human race was derived most commonly from her status as Mother of God (and consequently Queen of Heaven); it was derived most infrequently from the merging of her persona with that of 'pre-existent' *Sophia*; and it was derived quite often, but with a logical cogency that is seldom very clear, from such acts of Mary as her consent to her pregnancy with Jesus, her bearing and nursing him, and her com-passion with him on Calvary. But it is the nature of the role that is of interest, rather than the matter from which it is derived, and, as hinted above, the reason why all ambivalence about Mary's status must be removed from this role when it is not removed from the material from which that role is so often derived.

The most general feature of Mary's role in redemption are as follows: her maternal/queenly authority is such that God cannot really refuse her requests for mercy for sinners, and she has the added advantage that love and mercy predominate in her maternal character, where justice predominates in the Father God. As mother of the Son of God she can of course be said to have given the world its saviour, and that not merely because she physically bore him, but because throughout his life and hers she believed, followed and suffered with him, thus doing all in her power to further his work amongst people. Hence she can be said to have given her son for us, much as the Father did; she can be said to have defeated the devil, opened paradise, propitiated God—all through the work of her son. She can be said to be the channel of all grace to us. But, and this is the point of importance, no matter how strongly she is described as redemptrix, in that or equivalent terms, it is always made perfectly clear, either in the context or by the very next writer who comes along, that Jesus is the sole necessary and sufficient redeemer/mediator for the whole human race, and that her role is in consequence strictly intercessory or mediatorial in the quite restricted sense of channelling to us the necessary and totally sufficient merits of Jesus. Even the thirteenth century Richard of St Laurent, whose work on Mary achieved great influence when it circulated under the name of Albert the Great, when he describes Mary as omnipotent, quickly glosses such praise by explaining, 'she can do all things through the gift of her Son'.[10]

Why such assiduous qualification here, when ambivalence is allowed, and almost encouraged, in closely connected Marian contexts? I would not wish to allege a patriarchal plot, although I do think that a powerful, unconscious ploy is present, all the more powerful perhaps because it is unconscious. This ploy and the reason for it might be described as follows. A human being's primal encounter with the divine is through the twin threats of finitude and evil or, more precisely, through the awareness/hope of the presence of some power that can avert the twin threats. Cowed by the threat which death constantly poses to our finite, limited selves, further distressed by the dissolution which evil, both moral and physical, promises, our most original, powerful and formative encounter with the divine is in the experience/expectation of whole-making, healing power. In short, God the saviour is the first God we meet, in whatever form, and the last God we will want to know. Put in more theological terms, soteriology, the theology of saving power, its nature and processes, is the source and the serious centre of all theology at all times and in all of its history and evolution. It is, then, when people talk about salvation from the twin threats of finitude and evil, that they talk most seriously about God; it is then that they can afford the least ambiguity or looseness, characters of language which they might otherwise employ to good advantage.

Take this argument a stage further. Apply it to the role, noted at the outset, which religion plays as the ideological support of received social structures. It is the picture of the divine as effective (saving) power, itself the serious source and centre of theology, that is immediately relevant to the support of social structures, themselves embodiments of effective power in society. And this point is valid whether one takes the reductionist direction of our opening argument or its opposite. I mean, even if 'religion is nothing other than' a fantastic personification of powers inherent in social institutions and processes, it will be the soteriological heart of that religion's theology which will tell the true story, give the true reflection of the social powers, and other aspects of the same theology will prove more peripheral and subservient. Or, if we read the opening argument as I would want to do, in the opposite direction: it is the effective (saving) power that we see or wish to see embodied in particular institutions and processes in our society that shape our images of the absolute saving power we wish to see and then to appeal to in the universe as such. Consequently, when one is dealing in soteriology, one cannot afford to be ambiguous or vague, and one usually manages to be neither. Whereas when dealing with more peripheral and subservient matters, ambiguity may be advantageous in that it could prevent any clear challenge to the centre.

What I am suggesting then is this: any society will feel the need to represent the feminine at the level of divinity (or at the highest level of whatever secular ideology it substitutes for religion), for the feminine represents half of the reality in and through which the salvific process, however that is conceived, is expected to work. But in a society in which all effective power is in the hands of men, and it is intended that it should remain so, the image of the divine feminine will be at best ambivalent, the clear soteriological centre of theology (or ideology) where all effective agency is exercised will be a male preserve, and the very ambivalence of the language suggesting the divinity of the feminine in the peripheral areas of theology will prevent a challenge to the clear centre both by anticipating claims for divine status for the feminine and by doing so ambivalently and away from the centre. The woman will thus be represented at all the proper levels, but will remain in an essentially powerless, ineffective and subservient role. Christians have given themselves few opportunities of dealing with the feminine side of divinity; the Roman Catholic tradition has done so through its treatment of Mary in the ways outlined above; but it has done so in such a way as to secure patriarchal social structures.

The thesis that Mary is not allowed any genuine share in divine attributes where such a share might really count—in the divine process of saving the race—and that this is due to the (perhaps unconscious) working of patriarchal interests, is borne out by the general manipulation of Marian imagery in the Church. Marina Warner's book, *Alone Of All Her Sex* has already argued the general case that the cult of Mary has served to lower the status of women throughout the centuries. I do not wish to assess or to duplicate the general thrust of that argument here, but simply to choose some examples of the manipulation of Marian imagery most relevant to the analysis already conducted.

Take first the image of virginity. Mary is the Virgin Mother of God. Virginity is taken to signify openness to limitless possibilities, and fidelity.[11] All images, metaphors and symbols are based on some actual state of affairs, from which the range of significance is then extended, often in quite creative or poetic fashion, so as to bring to light a greater range of actual or possible experience. Virginity, as an image or symbol, has its base in a genital sexual state, and it symbolizes closedness, if anything at all, certainly not openness; and the failure so far to realize any possibilities whatever. It forces imagery beyond the range of intelligibility to suggest otherwise; and it borders upon the perverse to choose the virgin rather than the married woman as a symbol of fidelity.

Such blatant abuse of the natural range of image and symbol reveals some quite massive ideological pressure, for we have here almost, if not quite, reached the same level of distortion as Reagan reached when he described some obscene weapon of destruction as 'the peacemaker'. From where does this pressure come? Partly from the Church's misguided policy of declaring virginity superior to marriage.[12] Partly, and more importantly in this context, from the Church's efforts to keep women in their place. For Mary, the Pope declares, shows how virginity as a vocation for women in particular can be better understood.[13] The logic seems to be as follows: virginity signifies openness and fidelity (wrong); it also represents a superior Christian state (wrong as a generalization, which of course is what it is); so the way for women to achieve the superior Christian state is to remain virgins. So far so good, a simple if misguided piece of logic.

At least up to this point it is a misguided piece of logic which could be applied as much to men as to women. But there is a sinister extension to this misguided piece of logic, which can apply only to women, and which is so shaped as to deliberately exclude women from all effective power in the Roman Catholic Church where such power is altogether concentrated in clerical, hierarchical hands.

The extension of the misguided logic is as follows. The virgin, feminine at this point, open and faithful, and superior to married peers, is now represented as spouse to a physically absent, heavenly husband, Jesus. Marriage to this absent husband is one way of ensuring virginity on earth, if anything can ensure it, while offering some consolation for missing out on a real marriage;[14] but it is the further abuse of the spouse metaphor for Jesus in this one-to-one relationship with individual nuns which now calls for comment, for it is now combined with another, quite legitimate use of the spouse metaphor (Jesus as spouse of the Church), and all of this in order to justify the unjustifiable, viz. keeping women out of the priesthood. Because the spouse of the Church is male, it is argued, those who represent or image Christ to the Church, particularly during the central liturgy of the Church, the Eucharist, must be male. That is the main, repeated papal argument for rejecting women priests: those who image Christ to the Church, who are thus his *eikon*, must be male like him.[15] But this argument is supported by the use of the spouse imagery for the nun, and it can hardly be unwitting support: if the nun is Christ's spouse and the Church is Christ's spouse, she cannot represent Christ to the Church; she could not be Christ's image or *eikon* to the Church without representing herself as her own husband! Hence, women who enter the higher state of virginity can be nuns, but not priests.

The *eikon* argument itself has a long and discreditable history. Based on a patriarchal ideology which made the image of God consist primarily in *logos*, the intellectual principle in humans, and on the persuasion that women were inferior in intellectual principle to men (and supported by a primitive gynaecology which made the female foetus an imperfect male), traditional theology from the Patristic age made man the proper image of the saviour God, and women subsequently subservient in the scheme of salvation. Hence only males can be representatives/*eikons* of Christ towards the (rest of the) Church. This argument on its own is easily rebuffed nowadays by pointing out, for instance, that it is *logos/sophia* which is incarnate according to Scripture, in Jesus, and *logos/sophia* being beyond gender as male/female cannot support any preference for males as representatives or images of the saviour. Hence the usefulness of the ploy of placing the only women contenders for hierarchical power in a Church which insists on celibacy for its hierarchs, the celibate women or nuns, in the position of spouses of Christ who is himself spouse of the Church. Female virgins, images of Mary, can represent the Church (also called, a little incongruously, both virgin and mother of her spiritual children), but they cannot then represent Christ the saviour to the Church.

This extension of the misguided logic of manipulated Marian imagery shares with all other reasons for refusing women access to Christian priesthood the aura of special pleading, of selective presentation of available evidence, and of logical ineptitude. I hope I have shown in another context that there is in any case no evidence either in Scripture or in the early tradition for a priesthood different in kind and not only in degree, as Vatican II has it, from the common priesthood of all the faithful; so there is no point in these attempts to show that Jesus excluded women from ministerial priesthood deliberately and not just as an accident of cultural conditioning: since he never instituted such a priesthood he excluded no one from it.[16] What is of interest here, however, is that this ministerial priesthood, as it is called, has for long monopolized all the legislative, judicial and executive power in the Church, and women are thus totally excluded from exercising power in the Church while often being lauded for the very understanding of

Christian leadership as service, the very understanding on which Christian power should be modelled.[17]

Mary, then, is the model from the transcendent realm which tells women that they may aspire to the convent, but not to the hierarchy, and that that for them is the superior Christian vocation. Women's exclusion from the corridors of power is thus based on the extension beyond the original author's wildest imaginings of a marriage metaphor from an obtuse Pauline passage in which Jesus is described as bridegroom to the Church. But the same exclusion can also be supported from the more general picture painted of Mary, when that too is taken as a model for women in particular. Mary is mother of the Church in a way, yes, but in a way which proves she really is not mother at all, for the children she brings forth are 'conceived of the Holy Spirit and born of God', so that Spirit and God and not she do the real parenting.[18] She is model for the Church, yes: a faithful follower, disciple, example of what her son achieves, the coming of the kingdom; indeed, in the Roman Catholic doctrine of her Assumption, she is an exemplar of the glorious eschaton that awaits all of us, we may hope. Latin American Mariologists, it may be surprising to discover, do not go very far beyond this territory mapped out by papal documents. They lay more stress, of course, on the suppositions that Mary experienced poverty and exile, and on the fact that she experienced discrimination, but the only thing they seem to say she *did* about all of this was to sing the *Magnificat*, thus joining other prophetic voices, some of them women's, describing what the reign of her son could some day bring about. For the rest she intercedes.

Now all of this is very well and good. Disciples still on the way need models, especially ones who have already reached the distant goal. But none of this does anything in particular for women. Indeed, to give credit where credit is due, the present pope is a rather good apologist for women in general. He manages to get the very best from vaguely misogynist passages in Genesis and Paul, and to save Mary from what seem like slights from her son. The exegesis may be manipulative here also, but at least on this occasion the cause is a good one! And he does make much, not only of Jesus' consistent rebuff to conventional discrimination against women in his lifetime, but of the emerging portrait of women as faithful disciples, sources of confessions of faith at least as impressive as Peter's, and first witnesses to the risen Lord. He regrets that cultural conditioning prevents this to this day from having the ameliorating effect it should have had on the status of women. Yet he himself never seems to see the relevance it ought to have for the question of access of women to leadership in the Church. Through the light that Mary sheds on womanhood as such, he sees 'in the face of women the reflection of a beauty which mirrors the loftiest sentiments of which the human heart is capable: the self-offering totality of love; the strength that is capable of bearing the greatest sorrows; limitless fidelity and tireless devotion to work; the ability to combine penetrating intuitions with words of support and encouragement'.[19] But in none of this, as in none of the roles that women played in the ministry of Jesus and in the early Church, does he see anything that could give them access to ecclesiastical office. It seems odd to say the least, that such experiences and qualities should not qualify for hierarchical leadership in the Church, when mere maleness is absent.

The Church will be no better than it is, and it will provide no more effective leaven than it now does in society at large, until the present forms of clerical/hierarchical domination are radically changed. The critical demolition of the argument which excludes women from ecclesiastical office may well prove to be the beginning of a radical revision of the present ideology of a clerical hierarchy; and the successful practical prosecution of the case for the presence of women in all parts and levels of the Church might well be the beginning of a renewed Church.

This could all happen provided two conditions are fulfilled: first and most obviously, provided that women do not try to force themselves into ecclesiastical, and particularly into priestly, office with the same understanding of these offices which presently prevails, replete as that understanding now is with clericalism and authoritarianism. That would merely compound present problems and leave the Church still preaching messages to modern peoples which it itself signally fails to learn. People will only be preached to by those who practise what they preach.

Second, and more to the point of this article, a Church in which women are as at home and as effective at all levels as men now are will need a theology which secures the place of the feminine in the divine. Marian theology has been used traditionally in the Roman

Catholic Church in order to do this, but then the ensuing imagery was consistently manipulated in order to secure a subservient role for women in the earthly society of the Church itself. Perhaps Mary, the very human mother of Jesus is the wrong foundation on which to try to build the image of the divine as feminine. There is reason to suspect that whenever Mary did take on divine attributes, it was because, as two women theologians of Latin America put it, she 'has entered into different human cultures, she has met their deities, has influenced them and been influenced by them', and some of these were females.[20] It might then be as well to stop flirting with the divinity of Mary altogether, and to go back to the primal sources of all our religious consciousnesses in order to recover a fuller appreciation of the feminine nature of God.[21]

I know that there are strong suggestions, again made principally by Marxists, that although religious or ideological imagery and social structures mutually secure each other, change can come about only by starting with the latter and not with the former. I must say that when I recognized the validity of the eucharistic ministry outside my own Church, and within that ministry experienced the exercise of eucharistic presidency by women, I found a religious experience that liberated for me forms of the Spirit of Jesus hitherto locked away from me. And I should be happy to advise my fellow Roman Catholics to seek out such experience—it is sometimes available in hidden places in our own Church. But I am still sufficiently committed to theology to believe that the intellectual critique of present structures and the imaginative effort to renew the symbolism of the divine being that we believe to be active in our world can have its own efficacy, that it need not await concrete action on social structures, but that it can, if not precede these with any efficacy, at least accompany them, guiding and inspiring them.

I do know of one area of Christian literature in which Mary did reach truly divine status, and that in the efficacious process of redeeming the human race. This was in the poetry of the bards, a poetic establishment that lasted in Ireland from the twelfth to the seventeenth century and in Scotland for a century or so longer. In this poetry Mary did actually and positively contribute from her own merits to the saving of poor sinners threatened rather than saved at the Last Judgement by the cross of Jesus.[22] Why, you

113

might ask, did this not have any practical effect upon prevailing patriarchal policy? Because, I suppose, though poets are the most likely to discern the feminine face of whatever divinity there may be, they too are rendered peripheral by the power games played in most recent stories. As Patrick Kavanagh put it:

> While men the poet's tragic light resented,
> The spirit that is Woman caressed his soul.

Notes

1. Michael P. Carroll, *The Cult of the Virgin Mary* (Princeton University Press 1986), reminds readers that in the age of the cult and the numbers of its devotees (four and a half million each year at Lourdes alone) the cult of Mary exceeds all other cults (Moonies, Hare Krishnas, etc., etc.) put together.
2. When theological colleagues argue that the deep prayer experience of, say, an Oxford nun, provides evidence of the existence and 'structure' of the Trinitarian being of God, and the structure revealed turns out to support Augustine, I am inclined to wonder if a similar argument would be allowed to succeed when the no-less-deep prayer experience is that of a peasant woman in the West of Ireland.
3. Pope John Paul II, Apostolic Letter *Mulieris Dignitatem* (1988), n. 4.
4. L. Boff, *The Maternal Face of God* (San Francisco, Harper and Row, 1987), p. 101.
5. Boff's treatment of Mary, it must be allowed, has precedents in both Eastern and Western theology. One Richard of St Laurent, for instance, talks of Mary much as Scripture talks of the Father and the Son: 'Our Mother who art in heaven', 'Mary so loved the world as to give her only son', 'she emptied herself, taking the form of a handmaid'. (See Hilda Graef, *Mary: A History of Doctrine and Devotion* (London Sheed and Ward, 1963, I, p. 266). But an Eastern example shows that this could be regarded as no more than an example of *communicatio idiomatum*, a convention by which acts and passions of the human can be attributed to the divine (traditionally in Christ) without eliding the differences between them. See Theophanes of Nicaea, roughly of the same period as Richard (Graef, I, pp. 338–9).
6. Boff, op. cit., p. 95.
7. E. Benz, *The Eastern Orthodox Church* (Chicago, Aldine, 1963), argues that Orthodoxy, unlike Western theology, never merged *Sophia* with Mary. I doubt this. Certainly medieval Eastern theologians talked of Mary's pre-existence, of her being mother of the creator, co-creator, in language reminiscent of *Sophia* (Graef, op. cit., I, pp.

344ff.; see also Boff on Evdokimov, op. cit., pp. 95–6).

8. Graef, op. cit., I, p. 173.
9. Graef, op. cit., pp. 130ff., 167, 198–9.
10. Graef, op. cit., I, pp. 266–9.
11. Pope John Paul II, Encyclical *Redemptoris Mater* (1987), n. 5. See (surprisingly) Ivone Gebara and Maria Clara Bingemer, *Mary, Mother of God, Mother of the Poor* (Burns and Oates 1989), pp. 99ff.
12. *Mulieris Dignitatem*, n. 22. This mistaken view is dependent upon a confusion of celibacy with virginity, and on an attempt to extend the very impressive spirituality of the monastery to the world at large. Realization of the simple fact that successful extension would bring a quick end to the human race, results in recommending this spirituality as an ideal which it is assumed few of us can attain. But the mistake is made in generalizing this spirituality in the first place, as is done when virginity is declared *simpliciter* to be a superior vocation. There are folk outside the monastery who must forego family for the sake of some unusual service they are called upon to provide for the kingdom of God. All that can be said is that celibacy is best for those, and for those for whom the monastery or convent is best. It is not best, or superior, and quite possibly not even good for the rest of us.
13. *Mulieris Dignitatem*, n. 20.
14. One cannot but feel for a number of poor nuns who have undoubtedly been reduced by this strange logic to fantasizing (in a non-sexual, or at least a non-genital-sexual manner, of course) about a heavenly lover when they would be far better off both spiritually and mentally, not to mention physically, with some ordinary man, and relieved of that sense of rivalry which is the Hollywood version of the relation of divine love to human.
15. *Mulieris Dignitatem*, n. 26, repeating Paul VI in his *Inter Insigniores*. Needless to say (or is it?), it is a complete and dangerous distortion of the New Testament to suggest that priests are *in persona Christi*, even at the Eucharist, in ways in which others are not. The New Testament is perfectly clear about the fact that all human beings, but more especially the poor, the imprisoned, the hungry and thirsty, are for us so-called Christians the very *persona* of Jesus. That is clear from Matthew's great judgement scene, from the Pauline imagery of the body of Christ, from the Johannine theology of the love of God and neighbour. It is just too ubiquitously clear to allow any more distortion.
16. See J. D. G. Dunn and J. P Mackey, *New Testament Theology in Dialogue* (London, SPCK, 1987), chapters on church ministry. See *Mulieris Dignitatem*, n. 26.
17. See *Mulieris Dignitatem*, n. 5.
18. *Redemptoris Mater*, n. 5.
19. op. cit., n. 46.
20. See Gebara and Bingemer, op. cit., p. 18. It is interesting to note that the one appearance of Mary which these authors call properly

115

supernatural was at Guadalupe, the pilgrimage site of Tonantzin-Cihuacoatl, the serpent-mother-goddess of the native people to whom and on whose behalf Mary now presents herself.

21. In the actual sources of primal religions available to us (in these islands Celtic sources) the images of the divine female will already have been manipulated for patriarchal purposes. So anything we may find may have to be restored to its true value; but at least we should then be dealing with real deities rather than a human woman vaguely and inconsistently deified by default.

22. James P. Mackey, 'Mary in the Religious Poetry of the Bards', forthcoming in the next issue of *Cosmos*, Edinburgh University Press.

7 Women, ministry, and 'apostolicity'

I write in the Methodist tradition, as a member of a Church which decided to ordain women to the priesthood a generation ago, has done so, and does not seem to have suffered the divisive, destructive effects that are frequently assumed to have happened elsewhere—in Scandinavia, for example. In this absence of conflict Methodism is no more remarkable than the British Free Churches in general, which have taken this particular change as an unbuckling step towards the greater equality of the sexes, and as a recognition of what women have already contributed to the life of their Churches. I mean, quite seriously, that no great emotional investment was involved, either for or against a proposal which in Anglican terms is sometimes presented as though it would mean the end of religion in our time.

In the Methodist case—the one I understand the best—the phrase 'apostolic ministry' has never been the catchword of a group, nor has 'ministry', in the broader sense, ever been identified exclusively with the masculine. John Wesley judged 'apostolicity' in terms of faithfulness to doctrinal (he would have said Anglican, doctrinal) standards: he took it for granted that the teaching of the Church of England, evangelically (and not Calvinistically) under- stood, was 'apostolic'. He also measured 'faithfulness' partly in terms of effectiveness, asking if God honoured what was preached or otherwise taught by conversions or other signs of spiritual fruitfulness. These attitudes constituted a pragmatic test which made it hard for him to reject altogether the collaboration of women. I do not mean that John or his brother, Charles Wesley, both of whom were regularly ordained Anglican ministers, considered the formal ordination of women a possibility: Charles steadily resisted as totally improper John Wesley's willingness himself to ordain the Wesleyan itinerants, all of whom were male. But both men accepted the role of women as pastoral advisers and spiritual leaders; John found it difficult to say that women should never preach, as long as they did not actually call it preaching.

Indeed, eighteenth-century Wesleyanism at the local level—and it was the local level which mattered—was as much the creation of

117

women as of men. Women could, it is true, play an important role in eighteenth-century Anglican Evangelicalism, but the existence of women class-leaders, who had a pastoral role but were not ordained, gave a more formal value to their position in Wesleyanism. Even in 1968, when the official, ill-fated scheme for Anglican–Methodist unity was produced, the Methodist leaders had to be careful to say that their future acceptance of the 'strictest invariability of episcopal ordination' would not commit the Methodist Church to the view that the historic episcopate was essential to the apostolic character of the Church, and that this character was something which nonepiscopal Churches necessarily lacked. There had to be a saving clause for pragmatism, because a pragmatic attitude to questions of church order was the fundamental presupposition of the eighteenth-century Wesleyan movement. Not all modern Methodists rejoice in the pragmatic origins of Wesleyanism, but they cannot ignore them altogether. Indeed, it was a pragmatic fact that in the 1970s many Methodists were offering to accept episcopal ordination for the sake of unity, not unity for the sake of episcopal ordination, or for some kind of fresh guarantee that Methodist ministers were, after all, in an 'apostolic succession'. It is equally clear, I think, that having once tested the ordination of women in practice and found it acceptable, the Methodists will not worry very much about Catholic opposition. There may be cultural elements involved, but whereas an older generation of Methodists had found the presence of women local preachers, who conducted non-sacramental services in local chapels, something of a problem, there was no similar reaction against women presiding at the Eucharist. It is an additional example of the pragmatic tradition that women had in fact already been conducting eucharistic services for many years as Methodist 'deaconesses', that is, without formal ordination but with the specific authority of the Methodist Conference.

Methodists, therefore, find Anglo-Catholic objections to the admission of women to the priesthood hard to follow. 'Apostolicity', after all, was a mark of authenticity put forward in the early Church as a way of distinguishing local churches which had been founded in some kind of continuity with the apostles from other churches which showed heretical trends. In the sixteenth century large-scale division inevitably gave the idea fresh prominence, and while Roman Catholics put their stress on the possession of an episcopal succession from the apostles, the Reformers asserted that they were reviving a theological continuity with the apostles and the primitive Church which had largely disappeared in recent centuries. The difference between the two could also be thought of to some extent in terms of 'tradition', on the one side, and 'Scripture' on the other, both of which depended on apostolic authority. An 'apostolic' ministry, therefore, was one which claimed to be faithful to the essential witness of the apostles, and there was an obvious need for some such idea, and for some such institution, if Christianity was to remain visibly what its founders had intended.

However, by the time that the Reformers had established themselves it had become clear that the idea that Christianity must maintain an essentially unchanged, apostolic identity was ambiguous: it could be used to object to any kind of change, on the ground of loss of identity, or it could be used to defend innovation, on the ground that what was proposed expressed the true spirit of the apostles. This situation caused great anxiety in the sixteenth century, and again in early nineteenth-century Anglicanism, when John Henry Newman and his friends agonized over the where-abouts of the true, 'apostolic' Church. Yet again in the late twentieth century Anglo-Catholics and Anglican Evangelicals are both anxious about a loss of the Church's identity, though they don't necessarily define it in the same way. One has to recognize, in any case, that the apostolic identity, even when defined as episcopal succession, is primarily to be found in the whole life of the Church, and that the particular form in which we have received the church's ministry is a sign, not the substance, of the apostolic witness as such. It is truer to say that there have always been ministers of some kind in the apostolic succession than it is to say that these ministers have always been male.

This conclusion may sound perverse, but one has only to consider the history of the ecclesia. A few examples must suffice here. In the medieval period, for instance, Catherine of Siena dominated the western Church in her lifetime; in the seventeenth century the Inquisition worked hard to destroy the religious credibility of the iron Teresa of Avila, but those who study her today waste little time on the Inquisition's views. In the early nineteenth century, Elizabeth Fry, who had no doubt that she stood in the succession of the apostles, firmly rejected the 'modern' penitentiary prison system which was supported by many masculine ordained chaplains, and was certainly nearer to the mind of Jesus in doing so. And if one looks for traces of that great succession in more recent years, I think that one would pass over the male and usually ordained theologians, and rest on another gallant, tragic Carmelite, Thérèse of Lisieux, and the unofficial patron saint of the 'almost christians', Simone Weil. The official Churches may have wanted an authoritarian, male-dominated structure, but the existential Church, the only Church that can really be in the 'succession', has never been as gender-simple as that. There was always an unsatisfactory attempt at balancing, which meant that in practice women could organize Orders and run convents, could become deaconesses, could dictate whole spiritual traditions through their alleged mystical experiences: it is not so very surprising that in the end Wesleyan women became class-leaders and local preachers, and finally ordained ministers. The case would be complicated, but one could argue that this was an example of theological development within the tradition which has reached the point where the official Church has to accept what has happened. Even in the fairly limited case of the traditional male priesthood the relationship between the sexes has differed so much that one can hardly speak of an authoritative tradition running back to the apostles.

This becomes obvious when one looks at the ways in which the male priesthood, for which so much is claimed, has actually been developed. In the Roman Church, theory requires a celibate priesthood, but in the Orthodox tradition priests were left free to marry, as they were in the Church of England from the sixteenth century. The concept of the married priest has also shifted in recent times: at first the priest's wife was almost an anonymous figure; then she was transformed into a kind of married deaconess, who had to exhibit total loyalty to the ideal of the family while giving herself to the service of her church or parish—perhaps the extreme example of this was the relationship between Salvation Army married couples. In the past generation a sudden revolution has meant that the priest's wife increasingly refuses what is seen as a male-determined role and pursues, quite properly, her own identity in work not connected with her husband's responsibilities. It is rather late on in the day now to argue that one of these traditions is right and the other wrong: one has to look at the whole Church and recognize that there has been a great uncertainty about the nature of the priesthood and about the proper relationship of the sexes in that priesthood, an uncertainty which Protestantism, which had the historical advantage of disunity, was able to explore much further, though in the present-day Roman Catholic Church similar anxieties are reflected in the gulf, on the subject of priests being allowed to marry, between Hans Küng, for example, and the present Pope.

Küng is an interesting example of how uncertain the situation really has become. In his *Wozu Priester?* (1971), translated as *Why Priests?*,[1] he said that one could not say dogmatically that ordination to the priesthood was instituted by Christ: 'there is not the least proof of this institution'; and he went on to say that today ordination could no longer, as in the medieval period, 'pass as a sacral investiture, by virtue of which the receiver is . . . invested with a legal and sacral potestas that would enable and authorize him alone to consecrate the eucharist'.[2] Küng also said that the ecclesial ministry should not be exclusively male: 'in this respect the New Testament should be viewed as a time-conditioned work (remember the veiled women of Corinth)', and it should be interpreted on the basis of Paul's 'abolition' of discrimination between men and women.[3]

There are obvious criticisms of Küng's argument. If the New Testament is a time-conditioned document—and I entirely agree that it is—one can do no more with a quotation from Paul on this matter than point out that even in such a conditioned source surprising things could be said about the relationship of the sexes, but what Paul said can have no absolute authority, and it is obvious that he was not thinking about the ordination of women as such. Either the Church has a meaningful history or it does not, but that it has a history cannot be denied. And just as the New Testament is time-conditioned so is tradition, and so is our modern response to the problem of the ordination of women. What we also have, however, is a, by now, highly developed set of practical examples of what it means to authorize women to behave as full ministers of the Church; we are not simply innovating in the dark, we are not simply responding to some fashionable current of 'liberal' opinion, we are watching a situation develop and trying to learn from what is happening.

What was significant about Küng's discussion was that in the Roman Catholic Church one already had an important theologian whose vision of priesthood as a ministry of leadership and service, open to both men and women, came very close to what had evolved on the broad plain of Protestantism. It is fashionable to ignore Küng, except when he happens to be writing in a more orthodox vein, but his views on this subject are not particularly individual, except in their Roman Catholic context; he is not a heretic here, rather an example of a tide of theological development. One can no longer claim an absolute authority for an appeal to what the New Testament says about the proper bounds of female identity, or the true nature of a Christian priesthood.

We are now so placed that certain experiments with the priesthood are becoming inevitable: they do not have to be regarded as done once and for all, any more than, as far as the Church of England is concerned, the original western celibacy of the priesthood was fixed once and for all. There are times when, to an observer trained in dissent, the Church of England seems to go too far in seeking to divest itself of any 'Protestant' origin, but however one words one's judgement on the Reformation in England it remains true that Anglicanism emerged from the sixteenth and seventeenth centuries as a reformed Church, not as a Church of the Counter-Reformation. It was possible then for the Church of England to experiment with a married priesthood, to allow the dangerous presence of the sexual to come close to the sanctuary, to move, so to speak, from the presbytery to the vicarage: a stage in development was accepted, and not many Anglicans would now want to say that Canterbury was wrong and that Rome, which retained celibacy with even greater intensity than before, was right. The reintroduction of celibate monasticism into the Established Church has not been the signal for a widespread demand for a return to the celibate priesthood. There have been experiments in the past, there is no reason why there should not be experiments in the present.

I have not attempted to press my position by means of modern feminist arguments about the New Testament text and the patriarchal nature of tradition, because I do not think that this was the way in which the Free Churches came to carry out their own experiments. It is true that Elisabeth Fry lived through the years of the first strong feminist campaign, in which French and American influences played a large part, but she was drawing on a powerful Quaker tradition of actively religious women, whose 'concerns' were as valid as those of Quaker men. She used a highly developed theological vocabulary which had been handed down to her, not the language of Mary Wollstonecraft. Similarly, in Methodism what counted most was the surviving knowledge that the eighteenth-century religious movements of which Wesleyanism was a part had been experimental by nature: there was the same culture of spiritual freedom as haunts the background of the Franciscan orders, and made it easier for them than for some other groups to respond to the initial Vatican II demand for change. This internal pressure meant that lay administration of the Holy Communion by both sexes was possible before the ordination of women was introduced. Feminism came later and helped to justify what had happened.

This brings us back to another important aspect of the question: the highly emotional argument that in the eucharistic service the priest in some sense represents Jesus, and that this representation has to be masculine, so much so that one cannot tolerate the presence of a woman at the altar. From this point of view, the priest acts *in persona Christi*, and where this phrase is interpreted in a literal way there is strong pressure to retain an exclusively male priesthood. Theologically, one can reply that it is the whole Church which in the first place embodies the priestly activity of Christ, from which it would follow that the ordained ministry represents the wholeness of the Church, which itself is both male and female, and that there is no case for restricting the visible symbol of priestly activity to a male presence. Here the conservative case, one suspects, depends upon a residual bitterness, not all male, about the changes in the relationship between the sexes which have taken place in modern western society since the French Revolution. It is no accident, anymore than it is a political necessity, that one of the first actions of a liberated Polish parliament should have been that its upper house passed a resolution in favour of the criminalization of abortion. We live in a society in which there goes on continually a deep-level struggle between masculine and feminine identity: we all contribute to it, and we all fail fully to respect the identity of others.

In the Free Church tradition, from whose point of view I am writing, the doctrine of the ministry never became deeply entangled in these socio-political struggles. A degree of insular provincialism helped. Even more important was the legal toleration from the early modern period of groups like the Society of Friends, into which George Fox and Margaret Fell poured their remarkable personalities, and which never quite capitulated to the dominance of the mainstream society or the Churches which it contained. Even in Scottish Presbyterianism the deviant habits of the Holy Fair limited the claims of the male ministry well into the nineteenth century. Methodism certainly shared in the male counter-revolution which we call High Victorianism, but it moved on and recovered contact with its dissident roots. In the Free Churches there was rarely found the degree of concentration on *who* was presiding at the eucharist that leads to a prizing of the celebrant's maleness as an important symbol. If there was more than a secular reaction to an accustomed service, it would have been to an unseen Jesus, a presence which could, in more recent times, be as firmly mediated by a woman as by a man, and by a married woman as by a married man.

The movement toward a better mutual understanding between men and women is one of the few positive aspects of the dark, bloody history of the twentieth century. Everything that matters in a religious tradition which is more than merely apostolic, which witnesses to Jesus himself, cries out for a recognition of what is trying to take place. The skies will not fall if women are ordained to the Anglican ministry. Indeed, the Church of England should avoid becoming like the House of Commons, which is still essentially patriarchal. What the Free Churches can say is that the ordination of women is no longer a question of making a daring experiment, but of doing what needs to be done. It is priesthood itself which needs to be approached experimentally, and perhaps transformed out of all recognition; but that is another question, which the ordination of women does not in itself solve.

Notes
1. Hans Küng, *Why Priests?* (London 1972).
2. ibid., p. 66.
3. ibid., p. 59.

8 'They make such good pastors'

Feminism has offered a huge pastoral challenge. It has not so much raised doubts about men's pastoral gifts or their monopoly of them; more importantly, feminism challenges us to look again at what it is to be a pastor.

After all, the discovery that women have pastoral gifts would not be particularly novel. They are in fact supposed to be especially able in that field; and much good it has done them. We have all been told how good women are as carers, and that they are intrinsically possessed of selfless devotion. So they look after elderly relatives more often than men and are, presumably innately, biologically, expert with children, and this we admire.

It is true that our admiration for these skills has not been reflected in the pay scales they attract; but if the skills are supposed to come naturally (unlike those needed to run a company or fly an aeroplane) that is perhaps not surprising. The market-place seems to have brought into being the state of affairs which the received wisdom about women would have led one to expect. Or maybe the theories offer convenient rationalizations for what the market-place has established; it makes little difference in practice which way round it is. The honour paid to the caring aptitudes of women may well be genuine, but honour does not get anyone through the supermarket checkout.

Nor is that its only disadvantage. The honour paid to caring gentleness leaves the recipient of that honour with a massive problem of what to do with her anger, her ambition, her drive or her rebelliousness — or a combination of them all. The effects of that repression on their mental health is something many women can tell us about, and many others convey the unmistakable impression that the effects have been so serious that they cannot even do that.

For the myth of women's pastoral gifts, however positive it sounds, and even however admiringly it is recited, is a myth of origins. It seeks, that is, to found the destiny of persons in their physiology; it roots what they have to offer to humanity in the construction of their bodies and makes it as unchangeable as the

125

colour of their eyes. To be trapped in a role that is not esteemed or valued may be a more obvious form of enslavement; but to be trapped by a myth of origins in a role that is apparently positive is still just as much to be trapped. To root a person's vocation in her biology is in itself an act of oppression, and to declare the vocation a high one is not so much a consolation prize, as simply a way of compounding the offence.

The linking of pastoral gifts to the sex of a person is a sophisticated form of palmistry. The theory says in effect that you can tell that a person is predisposed to caring, if not by the lines on their hands then at least by the evidence of the missing Y-chromosome. Like the theory that the fittest survive in the market-place, this myth of origins simply and conveniently says that things are the way they are because that is how they have to be.

This is not the place to describe in any detail the complex relationship Christianity has had to myths of origins of many different kinds. Certainly there have been many issues and many occasions when it has added to the burden such myths impose on their victims the further load of declaring that the myth has itself been revealed in the Word of God. Not only are their life possibilities biologically determined; but God has said as much and is owed gratitude and even worship for making their destiny so clear. That demeaning train of thought is often repeated, for example, as the Church of England groans its way towards ordaining women as priests and bishops.

The importance of this point is that it suggests that we need to be circumspect in our choice of the arguments we use in supporting the cause of women in the Church. By 'we' in this case I mean of course we men; it is hardly for us to tell women how to argue their case. But it will be a very dubious form of support that furthers the cause in the short term while retaining great destructive potential in the future.

So in this instance I should be very suspicious of any support for the ordination of women as priests and bishops that rested on our need to have the benefit within the ordained ministry of their particular—pastoral—gifts. We need a great variety of gifts, and therefore a great variety of persons; that is true. But if, because it makes good advertizing copy or looks as though it will win votes, we assent now to the notion that we are losing particular gifts by not having women in the priesthood we shall be colluding with the lie that is the reason for the mess in which we find ourselves.

Furthermore, if we use that argument now so as to win the vote, how shall we resist it when it reappears as a benign looking clause in specifying people for particular posts: 'The diocese has been very well cared for, but does now need a strong sense of leadership and direction; we should probably not be considering a woman this time round'; 'This parish is very demanding in the number of people it contains who need a high degree of personal care; it might be especially suitable for a woman.' No doubt the second half of those two specifications would not actually appear in print, if only because by then that might be illegal; but if we have repeated that argument when it suited us it may well be inscribed too deeply in our mind to be easily eradicated.

The truth is that it is a myth of origins that lies behind the constraints placed on women by the Church, and no myth of origins, however benign or admiring it may appear, will release them. The freedom and fulfilment of human beings rests securely only on two foundations: God's freedom to call whom God chooses and to give what God chooses to whomever God chooses; and God's love given in Jesus Christ who has secured for us the benefits of that freedom in the face of all human attempts to constrain it.

The emancipation of women, therefore, in the Church or anywhere else, does not rest on any supposed endowments which women may be alleged to have because they are women. They do not have to earn it at the bar of men's esteem (or for that matter of their own often damaged self-esteem); it is theirs by the same gift and grace that freedom has been offered to all humankind. So we men are called upon to prevent ourselves and our brothers from standing in the path of that freedom. We are to do that not because we have discovered in women some capacity we value or something we modestly concede they seem to do better than men; we are to do it because we recognize that freedom as being—for women as well as for men—God's gift.

That raises the question why a book by men seeking to oppose sexism in the Church needs to contain anything about pastoral ministry in particular. There might just as well be chapters on management capability, or sensitivity in leading worship, or theological learning or any other skills we associate with ministry in today's Church. Every sphere of ministry is, we believe, in principle open to women and men alike. Then if there is nothing especially feminine about the practice of pastoral care do we need to say anything about it here at all?

Experience suggests that we do. We need to make clear how the long tradition of sexism in the Church has affected those areas of ministry which are deemed to be women's special province just as much as those from which women are excluded. As a very clear example, we need to see how that tradition of sexism has distorted not just the pastoral care given by women, but also the way in which men have seen their own pastoral gifts and responsibilities. Indeed what happens in a community distorted by sexism is a distorted understanding of what the whole pastoral tradition is about.

Two experiences during my time on Tyneside, each lasting over several years, have as I now see it profoundly affected my understanding of the pastoral task; both have to do with the struggle against sexism. The Newcastle Ordination of Women group, founded by Jan, my wife, and two friends, used to meet in our house and became a more or less regular commitment over a number of years. Such groups are hard to sustain: a single issue such as the ordination of women arouses great weariness if it is constantly discussed; the repertoire of campaign tactics is inevitably limited, and attempts to widen the concerns of the group into other themes of feminist theology and spirituality were bound to risk its fragile unity.

Yet as I look back on that period of my life I am strongly aware of having been held in membership of a Church-on-the-way, and I can see there the foreshadowing of some future model for being Church. For me the group held promise of a kind that was missing in so much of the day to day life of the official Church whose liturgy and life claimed so much. That was so despite the fact that I held a ministerial position of considerable privilege and challenge, offering a good deal of freedom to explore new patterns and many opportunities which were both enjoyable and rewarding. The group, though beset by many very ordinary difficulties, found that its common life was affected deeply by the issue with which it was primarily concerned. Whether we wanted it to or not—some did and some did not—the group had to consider how the fact that it was a group for the ordination of women would affect its style of meeting, its way of worshipping and its exercise of concern for its members.

So without my choosing that it should become so, the life of the group became an extended study in applied pastoral theology. Even before women were ordained their ordination seemed to usher in in advance pastoral insights and practices which challenged the received wisdom of pastoral care in a male-dominated Church. That is not to say that we had any sense of having 'arrived' at a 'new style of pastoral care'; old patterns often reasserted themselves, and in any case the difference was elusive. But the grace of mutuality seemed intrinsic to our task. So also, we found we had to find ways of combining a strength of conviction with a gentleness of execution—qualities which elsewhere seem to pull in quite opposite directions.

In parallel with that experience, and quite outside the range of the Church and its life, was my membership of a small group of men convened for the specific purpose of helping its members respond more effectively and sympathetically to the women's movement. Its life and its style made it quite different from the other group; it was not part of any campaign, and I was the only Christian in it. Yet in a very similar way the issue with which we were dealing seemed to possess and transform our life together, so that it was possible to model new ways of being with each other and caring for each other.

The themes of mutuality and of the connection, rather than the opposition, between strength and gentleness were there too as in the other group; it was just as hard to sustain from time to time and just as frequently reverted to old patterns which had to be interrupted when we noticed them. In the process, however, amid the tears, laughter and friendship, there were frequent experiences of the healing of those memories of school playgrounds and sportsfields, of academic contention and driving ambition, which so often impede the growth of men's pastoral capacities. For me the meetings offered great illumination of past occasions of difficulty. They reinforced discoveries I had previously only been able to make in the much more private context of counselling. The political and personal commitments of the members of the group were very varied, and yet we all felt that the surrounding male dominance had damaged not just the women who were its primary victims but us as well.

These two groups, together with other encounters, have left me with two perceptions about the struggle against sexism and its relation to pastoral care. First, the immense difficulties experienced by many of my brothers in changing their own attitudes and behaviour, or even in accepting that they need to change, seem now to be quite ordinary and predictable; in fact I incline to be suspicious of those who claim that confronting sexism occasions them no difficulty. In putting these thoughts together I am aware of the extent to which the pressure of a different role and work-load (very male problems those!) leave me much less supported when former patterns reappear with painful regularity. I do not believe that men can respond creatively to the challenges that the emancipation of their sisters throws up unless they allow themselves to experience together the sheer pastoral grace which engagement with feminism makes available.

Secondly, I am sure now that the pastoral growth which comes from the struggle against sexism does not come from the fact that women are biological females and men are biological males; in this as in so many other areas, our struggle is not against flesh and blood. Our struggle is not with our biology but with our history. There are analogies here with the struggle against racism and other forms of discriminatory attitudes and behaviour. The truth is that what distorts our common life and stunts our capacity to pastor one another is not our actual differences—in this case as men and women—whether those differences are seen positively or negatively. Rather it is the shared history of oppression which forces its victims to develop to a high degree forms of solidarity and mutual support from which their oppressors are then isolated.

There can be no doubt, therefore, that it is pastorally essential that women are included as equal partners in the exercise of Christian ministry. But that is not because for some mysterious biological reason women are better at pastoral work and so we need them to offer those gifts. Rather it is because their being on the receiving end of sexism has enabled if not actually required women to develop rich resources of mutual nourishment and care which men need to share in for their own growth and healing. It is not femininity that men need in pastoral partnership, but sisterhood as a powerful solvent of encrusted layers of defensiveness.

Not surprisingly, this is a gift we find it difficult to receive. Yet it is a pearl of far greater price than we should gain by simply acquiring women priests and bishops and expecting them to be specially good at pastoral care. What is on offer—and it is God's offer—is experiences of sisterhood that have the capacity to change and redirect us all by bringing the sexually divided qualities of strength and gentleness into their essential harmony. Together we can purge our memories of those damaging legacies of injustice that have harmed women so much and in the process incapacitated men also.

In that healing process of engaging with sexism, I am sure that we shall at the same time find more creative ways of confronting our heterosexism too. It is no coincidence that the Church is having to struggle with the issue of homosexuality at the same time as it faces up to the emancipation of women in its own life. One legacy of sexual stereotyping is a defensive and merciless response to those who find that their bodies do not conform in their essential direction to what the stereotype requires of them. This essay is not principally concerned with the issue of sexual orientation; but if the experience I have described is in any way typical, men need to undertake a painful examination of what has been expected of them, and how far they have managed, and failed, to conform to it. Without question, part of that expectation is that they should be unambiguously heterosexual.

A just relationship between women and men will be grounded in God's free generosity. To seek it will involve for men a deep and wide-ranging metanoia, a taking into themselves of some pieces of the pain and opportunity which are meant to be the shared lot of humankind but which women have been asked to carry. That search has the capacity to change many things in men's lives; when women are included in all spheres of ministry we must not just rearrange some of the external symbols of status and still perpetuate the baleful division of labour into which our history of injustice has initiated us. That is no way to honour women's pastoral—and other—talents.

Where this brings us is to a critical aspect of pastoral theology in general. For God offers and demands good shepherding most of

Peter Selby

all in the 'non-pastoral' aspects of life. When we struggle against our sexism we are beginning to take seriously the prophets' requirement of Israel's shepherds to regulate the life of the community in ways that are just and true. Pastoring in that sense involves many things before it ever refers to the acquisition of those skills needed for picking up society's pieces and bandaging its victims; it has to do first with fair management, just leadership, enforcing the divine laws which protect the poor—in short, with 'men's work', with all the activities which men's history has handed to them, whether in home, workplace or government.

So when we examine all that is implied pastorally by the overcoming of sexism, it turns out that we have to look again at the limited agenda that has in the past been associated with pastoring. What has happened to pastoral care is that its scope has been largely confined to offering help to those who are society's victims. That constraint exactly parallels the artificial constraints which have been placed upon women. They too have had prescribed for them what are the areas of life with which they may concern themselves. So the main pastoral effect of admitting women as priests and bishops will be to remove an injustice from within the Church's ministry. From that development all, and not just those who experience life as victims, will derive hope and the possibility of a future closer to the heart of God's intention.

Here we arrive where sexism produces its strongest resistance to change. For whether we choose that it should be so or not, we are dealing with our perception of God, God's intention and nature. I have never personally been enamoured of the distinction between 'first order' and 'second order' questions, often used in the debate about women's ordination for the purpose of reassuring people that as an issue it was not too terribly important. It cannot after all be that unimportant, or else we should either have managed it a while back or else given up on the idea; I cannot make much sense of saying that something is not too important even though everybody on both sides of the argument thinks it is.

It is surely inescapable that something in our perception of God is at stake in the struggle for the emancipation of women in every area of life. That can hardly be in any sense secondary. So many of the categories which have formed us doctrinally and spiritually bear the marks of the unjust history of relationships between men

132

and women. Surely we cannot suppose that we can attempt to remedy that unjust history and leave our fundamental experience of God unaffected. All that from a human standpoint we speak of as the 'rights' of women is in fact grounded in God's unconstrained freedom to call and bless whom God chooses; so it must also be true that the way in which we experience the relationship between women and men reflects and moulds the way we understand God's nature and God's relationship to us.

Yet here, at the point many Christians believe to be the most dangerous to faith, is our greatest opportunity. Within the learning I have described earlier has been found the bringing together of a whole host of human capacities and weaknesses which the unjust relations between women and men have forced apart. Strength and the capacity for weakness, gentleness and the exercise of leadership, vulnerability and the taking of authority—these and many other disjunctions have to be reunited if the struggle against sexism is to proceed. They need to be reunited not just at the level of theory, but as the result of a process of personal and corporate self-examination.

Yet these disjunctions we have also located in the heart of God, whose loving judgement and vulnerable rule of the universe represent combinations of qualities we have often made it impossible for ourselves to conceive. As static qualities they are indeed mutually exclusive; but the processes of self-examination and reconstruction that we need in the struggle against sexism do give us the possibility of a powerful experience of the way in which those divergent qualities in fact enlarge and enrich each other.

In the end therefore what is to be reconstructed is not just the distorted relationship between women and men nor the division of labour between those who rule and those who care for the needy. Pastoral care has been our theme: what we find is that if we seek to change those unjust relationships we shall be able to engage with what is at the heart of pastoral care itself. In that process, furthermore, we shall be given a deeper insight into the character of the one who is our Shepherd; in God are united the qualities we have so mistakenly and for so many generations split off from one another.

The struggle with our sexism encounters great resistance precisely because it takes us so near to the heart of ourselves; it

133

seems to demand that we make the hard emotional journey through our own childhood and adolescence, the time when our understanding of masculinity and femininity were formed. At the same time we find not surprisingly that we are also required to allow our earliest images of God to be reshaped.

One of the strongest memories I have of the Tyneside men's group is of a conversation at a party with one of the other members, a committed socialist closely involved in the affairs of his party and in numerous campaigns. 'I think', he said, 'that there has to be some connection between what you are struggling to do in the Church and what I'm trying to achieve in the Party. The problem is that we can't really describe what we are about because all the words seem to belong to the very way of seeing things and doing things that we are trying to change.'

There is indeed a failure of vocabulary to describe a world of sisters and brothers unconstrained in their relating by the injustices of the past. We find ourselves driven either to speak negatively, of what will not be the case in such a world, or in vague and abstract language. But as we struggle towards such a world, there are experiences to be had which give us some clues about what it might be like. As I listened to my friend speak of a project for which there are no words, I had a sense that I should want to call it God's project. I was also convinced that even if I could not find any words to describe the process or the outcome of that project adequately, it was one on which my sisters, my brothers and I would know from experience along the way what it was to be cared for.

9 *Language change and male repentance*

1970: At a Methodist theological seminary in the United States, students are teamed in support groups, for mutual care. One such group comprises a woman and eight men. Returning to her apartment one day, the woman sees a plastic bag hanging on the door handle. Inside is human excrement from the men in her 'support group'. The attached note says, 'This is what you are full of if you think you can do a man's job.' Her colleagues refuse to take seriously her anger and distress. 'It was a joke', they say. 'How can you be so humourless?'

1987: I am talking to some U.K. United Reformed Church ministers about the habit-forming power of language. I note that when English-speakers argue, they often use metaphors drawn from combat—attacking, defending, shooting arguments down, winning or losing them—and that this metaphor system structures thought and behaviour.[1] Realizing that my imaginary arguer has been 'he' for several sentences, I switch pronouns. By accident or Freudian slip I find myself saying, 'I was attacking her weak points but she retreated and shifted her ground.' From a man in the audience, as automatically as in a litany, comes the response, 'Just like a woman'.

1988: Pennsylvania, USA. A Lectionary Group of United Methodist clergy is studying next week's Scripture passages. There are nine men and one woman. Some of the men make pointed remarks about their female colleague's appearance: how attractive she must be to men in her congregation, how they must enjoy looking at her body, her breasts. The woman is humiliated and angry. The other men are embarrassed, but silent.

1989: In Ontario, Canada, two Anglican priests are leading worship. In his sermon, the male priest refers to God as mother. Afterwards, an angry parishioner rebukes his female colleague for speaking thus. 'I wasn't preaching this morning', she replies. But the reply goes unheard, and the woman is blamed.

1990: The preacher uses inclusive language for women and men. But all is not what it seems. A baby girl is baptized. She cries. 'She must take after her mother's side of the family', he remarks (laughter). One of his sermon illustrations is about people who waste time and energy worrying about unlikely disasters. 'A married couple are in bed at night', he says, 'when they hear sounds of movement below. The man gets up, goes downstairs and meets a burglar, who makes him hand over the family silver. Then the man says, "Before you go, come upstairs and say hello to my wife. She's been waiting to meet you for thirty years."' (laughter, some of it uneasy). The humour stereotypes fearless-man/frightened-woman, putting women in their subordinate place.

1990: UK and USA. In the past eight months, six women and one man in ordained ministry have told me their childhood experience of gross sexual and physical abuse, by fathers, uncles, and brothers. Many were long unaware of their traumas. Only in middle life did they regain childhood memories and struggle with their primal, crucifying burdens of fear, shame, and betrayal. For decades they had prayed, 'Our Father in heaven', without knowing why the image of God as Father was empty or terrifying. Some theologians tell them that 'Father' is God's revealed name, the only name we may use, and explain that it must be emptied of all connotations of sexuality, male dominance and male abuse because it really means the infinite graciousness of God beyond gender. If my friends can't do as they are told and disconnect God-as-Father from Dad-as-Father, these theologians see this is a pastoral problem, not a reason for re-examining their theology.

Most of these stories came my way in the first eight months of 1990, as my troubador ministry took me from place to place. As outcrops of male behaviour, they reveal the underlying strata of sexism in the Church: overt dicrimination, deep scorn of the female and feminine, rejection of female experience, and the use of language (including 'humour') to belittle, ridicule and humiliate.

OBSTACLES TO LANGUAGE CHANGE

Why won't men change their language? Why do we persist with 'he-man' language, where 'man' and 'men' allegedly mean 'human beings in general', and a person of unspecified gender is called 'he' or 'him'? Why do we insist on speaking about God with male-authority titles, such as 'Father', 'King' and 'Lord'? Why don't we notice the offensiveness of our anti-female 'humour'? Many women also resist language change, but I am best qualified to talk about men. I see five overlapping obstacles to change:

1. *Gender-blindness.*

I am colour-blind.[2] I cannot see why friends get excited as their garden tree turns from summer green to autumn red. I begin to see only if I stand close and look hard. Many men (especially white heterosexual men) are similarly uncomprehending of language and gender issues, and have not stood close or looked hard. We have not *heard* articulate women (though we have probably met them). We have not experienced discrimination, felt the controlling power of other people's language, or connected our discomfort when laughed at with women's discomfort at our sexual innuendo, anti-female 'humour', and patronizing characterizations of them as 'The women, God help us!' or 'The ladies, God bless them!'[3] We build conceptual walls round our theologies, to prevent female theologizing entering the fastness and challenging our securities: we keep women outside the walls, and look over with pastoral concern. We don't know that we need to listen to women. Or we don't know how to listen. Or we don't want to listen. Like Major Bloodnok in the 1950s radio Goon Show, we hear unpalatable truths, and respond stoutly: 'I don't wish to know that!' We think male dominance is passing away, and women have little to complain about. We use theological anaesthetics, classifying rape, domestic violence, physical and sexual child abuse, and sexual harassment generically as 'sin', thereby avoiding the painful rethinking involved in naming these mainly male behaviours as *male sin*, rooted in our own male identity in patriarchal society.

2. *Cosmetic conversion.*

Some of us try to change our language, but our attempts are half-baked and half-hearted. 'It's a women's issue', we say. 'I do my best to change the way I speak, out of pastoral concern, but it's hard to avoid slipping up.' Wanting to listen is an important step, but doesn't go far enough. 'It's a women's issue' implies that it isn't an issue for us men. We have 'pastoral concern' for women, but are ourselves unconcerned. If left alone we'd go on talking about God the Father and the Brotherhood of Man. We become motivated to change only when we realize that male dominance and male-dominance language go hand in glove, and that rejecting one means letting go of the other. If we find it hard to stop saying 'mankind' or calling God 'he', the fault is not in our syntax, but in ourselves.

3. *Fear and flight.*

Beneath our rational exterior, I suspect many of us have fears and anxieties difficult to examine when we encounter feminism and feminist theology. As the poet Robert Bly observes, most men know what's happening in our bodies from the neck up and the waist down; it's the part in between we don't know much about. Its unmanly to admit fear, and our deepest self has been formed to control, overcome or deny it. So our fears may be so remote from consciousness that we hardly know what they are or how to find them. Are there, deep down, fears shapeless and nameless: fear of the female and feminine, surfacing as scorn, 'humour' and condescension; anxiety about family-and-work-roles as women claim power and move into formerly male territory; familiar fears of losing power and status; or strange fears of psychic death amd castration? Are we troubled because we lack a positive masculine self-definition? If we sense such fears, who do we talk to? Some of us talk to women, who caringly listen. Yet we remain unsatisfied, with anxieties unresolved and inadmissible in the academy and pulpit, or on the episcopal bench. Thankfully, some of us are beginning to talk to each other, dream dreams, tell stories, and meet the male within.

4. *Linguistic problems.*

Perhaps we are unaware of linguistic evidence or unconvinced by what we have heard. As men, we stand here on safer ground. We can ask if 'man' has changed its meaning, or look at problems of biblical translation. We can weigh evidence and try to reach conclusions.

5. *Theological issues.*

Similarly, we can explore questions such as, is God revealed historically, *through* Abba/Father–Son–Spirit language, or timelessly, *as* Abba/Father–Son–and–Holy Spirit? How do we decide?

The first three obstacles need the most work, but are beyond my scope and space. So I shall look briefly at linguistic and theological issues, focusing on recent discussions of 'he/man' language and language about God.

LANGUAGE ABOUT HUMAN BEINGS

There was a time when 'man' meant 'the human race', 'a man' was a male or female member of it, and 'men' were human groups of either or both genders. In Anglo-Saxon, a human individual was 'wer-man' (male) or 'wif-man' (female). Sometime around the ninth century, 'man' began to be used for male humans as well as human beings in general, though Aelfric could say of a convert's mother, without incongruity, that she was 'a Christian named Ellen, a full-of-faith man, and very pious.' 'Wer-man' dropped out of use (with 'wer' surviving only in 'werewolf'), and 'wif-man' became 'wo-man'.

Over the centuries, the dual use of 'man/men' became increasingly ambiguous. Though it persists, the evidence is that the male meaning is central and the generic meaning obsolescent. 'Man overboard' still means 'child, woman or adult male', but 'men working overhead' is ambiguous, while 'men only' means that women and children may not enter. If the words were fully generic, we could safely tell a class of teenagers that 'Man is a mammal, so breast-feeds his young.' Or we could say—

> All men are mortal.
> Socrates is a man.
> Therefore Socrates is mortal.

—and then substitute 'Julie' for 'Socrates' without incongruity. Often the ambiguity is sexist, as in Erich Fromm's, 'Man's basic needs are life, food, *access to females* etc.', an utterance which begins with the supposedly generic meaning and shifts gear in mid-sentence, showing that the speaker was thinking of male humans all the time. Intentionally or not, persistent use of the ambiguous generic suggests that male humans are normative, and females derivative.[4]

Once we reject the old generic, there are numerous alternatives. According to context, 'human being(s)', 'humankind', 'humanity', 'the human race', 'people', 'person', and sometimes also 'all' or 'us' can serve us well. Whether they sound elegant or not depends on the cadences of the utterance in which they occur.

Why, then, do some theologians defend the generic usage? In their recent book, the Bishop of London and colleagues see few satisfactory alternatives to generic 'man/men'. They concede that in the Nicene Creed, *di hemas tous anthropous* (Greek)/*propter nos homines* (Latin) means not males but human beings, so can be rendered otherwise than 'for us men'. Yet the concession is reluctant ('nothing would be lost' not 'much would be gained'). They also concede that *enanthropesanta* (Greek)/*et homus factus est* (Latin) can be correctly translated 'and became a human being' (instead of 'and was made man'), but say this translation is inelegant and misses a theological point. But their standards of elegance are not elaborated, and their theological point argues the advantage of 'was made' over 'became', which could be satisfied by translating 'and was made a human being'.[5]

Our three authors may cling to the old generics partly because they don't know the evidence for their ambiguity. They would find the linguistic evidence inconvenient, because their preference for 'man' is ideological. The reason for it emerges when they argue that the maleness of Jesus is essential to our salvation, and that only men can be priests. The old generics skate over the problems of this view: 'God became a man to save men' sounds more straightforward than 'It is because God became a male human being that women and men can both be saved but only men can be priests.' For the authors of *Let God be God*, it seems that male generics in credal statements are more male than generic, and are preferred because they express and sustain a view of the Church as a society led by male priests, where a woman can never expect to be treated as the equal of a man.[6]

LANGUAGE ABOUT GOD

In my book on God-language, I argued that the systematic use of male-authority images of the divine (King–Almighty–Father–Protector) distorts our knowledge of God and reinforces male dominance.[7] *Let God be God* holds that God has chosen such language 'to express to us the kind of God "he" is'. God is revealed to us *as* Father, Son and Holy Spirit, and bids us use these terms in prayer and praise. To cease using them means discarding God's revelation.[8] By this they mean 'cease using exclusively': male-authority language is God's language, and nothing else will do.

The authors argue that since the time, place and mode of the incarnation were God's choice, Jesus' naming/knowing God as Father is mandatory. They accept the dogmas of the Trinity and the person of Christ from the ecumenical councils between 325 CE and 451 CE as the theological structures through which they think and speak of God. According to these dogmas, divine and human nature are united in Jesus, enabling the eternal Word to speak timelessly through his history-bound words and deeds, including his experience of God.[9]

However, understanding the incarnation as God's choice does not dictate a particular view of God-language. If 'we have to discern what is of divine revelation in the record',[10] Father–Son language is as open to question as anything else. The ecumenical councils try to reconcile Hellenistic beliefs that divinity cannot change or suffer with the biblical story of God-with-us in a human being who is born, grows, suffers and dies. Though the documents are classic reference points, they are not timeless. Describing an uninvolved deity whose 'nature' becomes united with Jesus' human 'nature' is as culturally conditioned as other attempts to explore how God was in Christ, before and since.[11]

Though the authors notice Jesus' revolutionary attitude to women, it doesn't alter their theology. They observe how he stepped outside patriarchal boundaries by including Mary of Bethany in the circle of disciples, and may even be aware of female leadership in the early Church.[12] Yet they arbitrarily claim that the later, patriarchalized Church, with its hierarchical structure and male-only clergy, shows the timeless will of God. From the fact that Jesus knew God as 'Father' and taught his disciples so to pray, they jump to the assertion that this usage must be exclusive and everlasting.[13] They fail to see how *anti-patriarchal* Jesus was in his context, and reduce his injunction to 'call no man on earth "Father"', from a denial of patriarchal power to mild advice about forms of address.

The authors describe revelation in terms drawn from male dominance. It is said that God 'enters and *masters* the environment', that 'in Jesus, God *masters* human nature and overcomes sin and death' and that 'the process of *mastering* and transforming continues' as the Holy Spirit unites us with Christ and each other. Following scriptural precedent, this language is intended paradoxically, so that the 'mastering' of all creation is somehow achieved 'through the form of lowly service, suffering and sacrificial death'.[14] Yet instead of exploring this paradox the authors deploy a sustained rhetoric of compulsion and command. It is under 'the loving *compulsion* of the truth' that our language about God is formed. The evidence that God is revealed as Father, Son and Holy Spirit is 'overwhelming and compelling', and God's truth 'compels our obedient receiving of it'. We use revealed language 'under the compulsion' of the truth Christ is, and see 'the compelling light of revelation'. In order so to compel us, we are 'confronted' with God's self-evidence. The integrity of God's truth 'confronts us within our limitations'. Having confronted and compelled us, God's truth controls us. The terms and language we use about Jesus and God 'have to be *controlled* from the objective reality which is of himself', so that we obey the 'unavoidable implications' of revelation.[15]

As if expecting us to resist being compelled and controlled, the book calls up reserves of wordage to make us listen. For example, we must allow God to be '*exactly* what he *truly* is', because God has '*divinely* selected and *divinely* arranged' images like Father, Son and Holy Spirit, which are '*express* terms sanctioned by God *himself*, to which the New Testament *so eloquently* witnesses'. 'Father' is God's self-naming, '*and this we cannot ignore*'.[16] The message is reinforced with frequent warnings of heresy and apostasy if we interfere with the fine balance of the content of revelation.[17]

By using stereotypically male language of command and control, our authors reveal themselves as male theologians who seemingly haven't enquired how their maleness affects their theologizing.

The wagging finger of emphasis suggests the anxiety of an authority under threat. The gospel paradox of the divine Word exercising 'mastery' through 'vulnerability and tenderness'[18] ought to vex them more than it evidently does. For if vulnerability and tenderness are the norm, it will be less easy to justify hierarchical church structures, priestly dominance, and the command rhetoric of these three male authors. As for truth 'compelling us', why not speak instead of the beauty of God's truth, its fulness, attractiveness, fragrance, and healing power?

The authors have difficulty explaining why God mandates male-authority language for our praise, prayer, and thinking. They affirm that God is neither male nor female, and seek to set aside 'any view of God which suggests maleness or patriarchy or "crude sovereignty, lordship, power"'.[19] Our symbols 'only point to the truth, and are of themselves totally inadequate fully to describe and contain the truth'.[20] Yet 'the words "Father" and "Son" are . . . commanded by God',[21] and credal Father–Son language is in accordance with the nature of divine truth, pointing 'beyond itself to what the limitless and inexpressible majesty of the truth is'.[22] Similarly, 'the fact that the Word became male and not female is . . . an essential aspect of the incarnation'. The male Jesus was 'THE image of God . . . the only permissible image which is complete in itself'.[23] Only male priests can represent this essential aspect of God, for they 'point to Christ in symbolism and imagery appropriate to the mode of the incarnation'.[24]

Despite contrary affirmations, these arguments only make sense if God is in some way more masculine than feminine and women subordinate to men. If male-authority language is the only language in accordance with divine truth, it must express something about God which female images cannot do. If the irreducibly male Jesus is in his maleness the only complete image of God, it follows that maleness is the normative image of God and femaleness subordinate or derivative. Though male and female are bound in mutual respect and love, the authors see the relationship in terms not of equality but of 'complementarity'.[25] Though they don't say what this means, they leave enough clues. Their recognition of the intimate connection between the use of language and women's rights and status in the Church[26] implies that language use mirrors theology and power-structures. Co-equality of women and men in ministry would go with co-equal use of male and female metaphors for God, whose co-equal trinitarian relationships male and female are said to image.[27] Conversely, male-authority God-language goes with a male-only priesthood and a Church where women cannot be fully equal with men. Since this is what the authors want, it follows that 'complementarity' means subordination.

Let God be God's linguistic theory also fails to carry conviction. The argument is that the meaning of God as 'Father' is unconnected with human fatherhood. 'We just do not begin with the concept of fatherhood (in any time or culture) and apply that to God',[28] for 'what God intends by "Father" will be different from the understanding of the term "father" in any human culture'. When we speak of God as 'Father', language is stretched 'beyond those lexical and literal definitions' and 'beyond all normal dictionary meanings'.[29]

The authors are not consistent, for elsewhere they argue that Jesus' understanding of God 'gains meaning from the reality of human fatherhood in human society', that the presence or absence of human fathers affects people's grasp of the symbol, and that God is the source of human fatherhood.[30] They also invoke divine intervention. Our relationship with God is an imageless relation, and knowing God as Father is a relationship brought about by the Holy Spirit. Christ creates in our minds human terms which point beyond themselves, 'indicating more than they can specify and quantify'.[31] The problem is that in writing their book, these theologians have chosen to stand in the public forum and deal in matters which *can* be specified and quantified. Outside that forum, there is no room for argument, only acceptance or rejection of their authority. I shall remain in the forum, and examine their linguistic claims.

Taking these claims at face value, we are asked to believe that worshippers and theologians can apply the word 'father' to God without any connotation of maleness, male authority, or male parenthood. The unstated linguistic theory is that these terms can so be taught that they lose all connection with normal meanings and acquire meanings that are quite different. If our leaders tell us that God–Father doesn't mean X but rather Y, Z and P, we can let normal meanings fall away, and switch to the meanings determined from on high.

No evidence is presented to support this claim, which rejects the widespread view among linguists that meanings are determined by users and that language is a complex system not easily altered by pronouncements from authorities. As regards father-language, the claim is implausible. We are not dealing with a minor concept without emotive overtones, but with terms that resonate at the deepest levels of experience. The difficulties many people have with God as 'Father', and the fierce opposition of many others to any change in Father–God language, count against the view that 'Father' can be emptied of father-content. It is doubtful whether anyone can detach parent names — whether 'father' or 'mother' — from primal experiences and cultural stereotypes of parenthood.

Since feminists and anti-feminists alike understand God-as-Father partly from experiences of human fathering, *Let God be God*'s imageless relation is only achievable, if at all, by a liturgy of continuous translation: 'OUR FATHER (But I must remember that I don't mean a male parent-figure, whether abusing or caring, authoritarian or egalitarian, but a God beyond sexuality, beyond male, female, masculine or feminine, infinitely gracious and utterly reliable, who has mysteriously decided that this name suggesting male fatherly authority is the only name 'he' — though of course I don't really mean 'he' — wants us to use in worship), WHO ART IN HEAVEN, HALLOWED BE THY NAME . . .' 'IN THE NAME OF THE FATHER (pause for translation), AND THE SON (pause for translation) AND THE HOLY SPIRIT (pause for exhaustion), AMEN.'

The authors' case would be stronger if male-authority God-language stood out sharply from Church and culture. The persistence of Father–God language in a thoroughly matriarchal culture might be persuasive evidence that God wishes us to use it, as might the persistence of command–obedience language in an egalitarian church whose archbishop was noted for her humility, openness and collegial style. What we find, however, is male-authority language in a male-dominated Church defended by male clergy whose views imply that women are subordinate to men and that maleness is the normative image of the divine.

CALLING GOD 'HE'

In common with many theologians, the authors of *Let God be God* routinely use masculine pronouns for the divine. God reveals

145

himself through Father–Son language, and *he* bids us use these terms in our address to *him*.[32] This is problematic, because modern English uses pronouns differently from biblical languages.

Hebrew and Greek have *grammatical gender*. Though 'masculine' and 'feminine' pronouns often denote male and female gender, they frequently do not. The Greek word for 'house' is masculine, so its pronouns are masculine, but it would be incorrect to translate them with English masculine pronouns, so that your house becomes 'he'. Similarly,

> *Der Hund ist klein und er ist treu.*
> *Die Kohle ist hart, sie ist nicht weich.*

should not be rendered:

> The dog is little, and he is loyal.
> The coal is hard, she is not soft.[33]

This translation is incorrect because the German pronouns do not suggest sexual gender. English pronouns do. 'He' and 'she' mark the sexual gender of their antecedent nouns, while 'it' almost always refers back to animals or non-personal objects. Though nineteenth-century male grammarians tried prescribing English 'he' as a generic pronoun, they did not succeed. Nowadays, the masculine pronoun 'overwhelmingly tends to be comprehended as sex-specific (i.e. male), even in supposedly generic contexts and in contexts doctored to encourage the perception of females'.[34]

Thus, translating pronouns from Hebrew or Greek into English entails a choice absent from the original. In Hebrew and Greek, 'Lord' and 'God' are *grammatically* 'masculine', and the masculine pronoun is mandatory. In English, we must choose whether to call God 'he', 'she', or 'it', or avoid pronouns altogether. The grammatical 'masculine' in biblical languages does not mean that God is male, any more than the feminine grammatical gender of 'Spirit' in Hebrew means that the Spirit of God is female. When we translate into English, however, we enter a language world where every pronoun choice suggests sexuality. In this world, the effect of larding our speech about God with 'he', 'him', and 'his' is to masculinize God. Since God is not male, female or neuter, to avoid calling God 'he' is to speak correctly, or make a correct translation.[35]

It may seem incongruous to end a discussion of weighty issues by arguing over a pronoun. Yet such language changes are an essential part of our repentance from sexism and journey with God. Gail Ramshaw puts it well. If we meet again the God of the burning bush, the parting waters, and the raining manna, God the soaring eagle and mother hen, God our creator revealed in the cross, we will laugh at the inadequacy of calling God 'he' and resolve to be more articulate in our speech. For 'change of speech is a willing task if it follows a conversion of mind'.[36]

Notes

1. See my book, *What Language Shall I Borrow? — God-talk in Worship: A Male Response to Feminist Theology* (New York, Crossroad & London, SCM Press, 1989), p. 65 and the work there cited: George Lakoff and Mark Johnson, *Metaphors we Live By* (Chicago, Chicago University Press, 1980).
2. I have been made aware that 'blindness', meaning wilful refusal to accept truth, though a scriptural metaphor, is unjust to unsighted or partially sighted people because it equates disability with perversity. Since 'colour-blindness' describes my own minor disability, I shall use it, unless it offends or is shown to be unjust. Attention to language is not nit-picking, but professional ethics.
3. Dorothy L. Sayers, 'The Human-Not-Quite-Human', in Dorothy L. Sayers, *Are Women Human?* (Grand Rapids, Eerdmans, date not available), p. 47.
4. Data and examples from Shannon Clarkson, *Language, Thought and Social Justice* (New York, Division of Education and Ministry, National Council of the Churches of Christ in the USA) and Casey Miller and Kate Swift, *Words and Women* (London, Penguin Books, 1976), pp. 44–6.
5. Graham Leonard, Iain Mackenzie and Peter Toon, *Let God be God* (London, Darton, Longman and Todd, 1989), pp. 60–5.
6. *ibid.*, pp. 71–3, emphasis mine. 'God became a man to save men' and 'It is because God became a male human being etc.' are my illustrative phrases. *Let God be God* opposes the idea that a woman should be 'treated in all ways as the equal of a male person' (p. 71).
7. *What Language Shall I Borrow?* (See Note 1).
8. ibid., pp. vii and 5, emphasis mine.
9. ibid., Chapter 5 and p. 2.
10. ibid., p. viii.
11. On fourth and fifth-century Christian doctrine in its cultural setting, see Jürgen Moltman, *The Trinity and the Kingdom of God* (London, SCM Press, 1981), pp. 21–5 etc., and Frances Young, 'A Cloud of

Witnesses', in *The Myth of God Incarnate*, ed., John Hick (London, SCM Press, 1977), pp. 13–47.

12. See Elizabeth Schüssler Fiorenza, *In Memory of Her* (New York, Crossroad & London, SCM Press, 1983).

13. For Jesus' use of 'Father', see *What Language Shall I Borrow?*, pp. 183–8.

14. *Let God be God*, pp. 10–12, emphasis mine.

15. ibid., pp. 5, 9, 18, 19, 20, 30, 38–9, 45, and 56, emphasis mine.

16. ibid., pp. 27, 31, and 48.

17. ibid., p. 56.

18. ibid., p. 75.

19. ibid., pp. 4 and 75.

20. ibid., pp. 20, 30, 39 and 46.

21. ibid., pp. 31 and 33.

22. ibid., p. 20.

23. ibid., pp. 29, 32 and 46.

24. ibid., p. 72.

25. ibid., pp. 22–4, 29–30 and 65.

26. ibid., pp. 65 and 27. The authors affirm that 'it is not the male without the female or the female without the male which is the image', and that the male–female relationship 'images in a temporal fashion the existence of the eternal God as Father and Son in the bond of eternal love which is the Holy Spirit'. (pp. 74 and 47–8). Since the persons of the Trinity are co-equal, this ought to imply co-equality of women and men, and the equal ability of female terms and metaphors to reveal the divine. The authors either don't follow their own logic, or have a subordinationist view of the Trinity.

28. ibid., p. 53, also pp. 54 and 73.

29. ibid., pp. 5 and 56–7.

30. ibid., pp. 54, 57 and 75–6. Apparently, God is not the source of human motherhood.

31. ibid., pp. 46–7, 76 and 38–9.

32. ibid., p. viii, etc.

33. Example from *Heute Abend*, a German Grammar by Magda Kelber (London, Ginn & Co., 1983/1962), p. 6.

34. Philip M. Smith, *Language, the Sexes and Society* (Oxford and New York, Basil Blackwell, 1985), p. 52.

35. See Burton Throckmorton, 'Language and the Bible', in *Religious Education*, Vol. 80, No. 4 (Fall 1985), pp. 523–38 esp. pp. 535ff.; Elizabeth Schüssler Fiorenza, *In Memory of Her*, pp. 43–8; and Gail Ramshaw, '*De Divinis Nominibus*: The Gender of God', in her book, *Worship — Searching for Language* (Washington DC, The Pastoral Press, 1988), chapter 19, pp. 189–204.

36. Gail Ramshaw. '*De Divinis Nominibus*'. p. 203.

MICHAEL JACOBS

10   *Is anatomy destiny?*

The aphorism 'Anatomy is Destiny'[1] was coined by Freud. It might also have been seized upon by those in the Churches, who have appeared to argue against the ordination of women on the grounds that women have been created almost as a sub-species, and are physically not suited to the functions of priesthood. Nevertheless, outdated as such an argument might seem to the liberal and so-called progressive thinker, or to the male who has become conscious of the issues about sexism (sometimes known as the 'New Man'), 'anatomy is destiny' is not a phrase which can be readily dismissed.

Freud had more trouble with the phrase than is apparent from the two places where he employs it. The words are of course a convenient way of describing that there are clear differences in the way in which young girls and boys develop in that stage of child development that has been characterized (though not exhaustively described) by Freud's term 'the Oedipus Complex'—the rivalrous relationship between the child and both parents. Freud suggested that the presence or absence of that part of the anatomy which in one gender includes a penis, and in the other a vagina, spelled anxiety about castration in little boys and envy of the penis in little girls. But though anatomical difference clearly means something to children, it is not necessarily solely or universally what Freud thought.

While we may have more metaphorical ways of understanding castration anxiety and penis envy than Freud did, his own difficulty was less apparently with such questions in childhood. He appears to have had more trouble in working out how to view adult women and men. He seems both to encourage and yet to denigrate women; and to reject, yet also to support, the idea that men and women are different. It is this contradiction in him which acts as a pointer and parallel to what is essentially just as much an issue for our own time, when quite a number of women and rather fewer men are trying to understand the concepts of feminism on the one hand, and masculinity on the other. (It is worth noticing from my juxtaposition of these two nouns that there is already a difference as well as something in common. Femininity is not nearly so acceptable a term to feminists, and masculinism seems not yet to exist.)

It is therefore salutory to pursue Freud's dilemma further, because although he was not a 'New Man', towards the end of his working life he obviously had to struggle and try to come to terms with the contribution and the criticism made by women colleagues. In that sense he prefigures for us some of the struggles within the Churches, as men in positions of influence and power accommodate to the fuller entry of women into their profession.

In Freud's Introductory Lectures[2] in 1917 and in his New Introductory Lectures[3] in 1933 he recognized an audience composed of 'Ladies and Gentlemen'. Certainly by 1933 women were playing a significant part in psychoanalysis. But the 'Ladies' whom he addresses, if we look beneath the surface, might just as well be honorary men. In a useful, although patchy essay on 'Femininity' in the same New Introductory Lectures he acknowledges the value of the contributions made by women analysts to the understanding of the psychological development in girls. He observes that they criticized the male analysts for being prejudiced in their researches, in making unfavourable comparisons between men and women. Then he gives the game away: 'This doesn't apply to you. You're the exception; on this point you are more masculine than feminine.'[4] Such sexism assumes even greater seriousness when it is translated into psychological theory, such as the phrase a few paragraphs later where he discusses a girl's aggressive impulses as being on a par with those of a little boy: 'we are now obliged to recognize that the little girl is a little man.'[5]

Women (or some women) are therefore not any different from men: they show themselves as being as capable as men; or perhaps Freud is really saying that when they behave in ways which he admires they are in fact behaving more like a man. If we pursue other somewhat more sympathetic hints about women in his writing (largely stimulated by what women analysts were writing about the psychology of women and girls), there are less patronizing statements that also suggest that women are in fact no different from men (or perhaps we should say men are no different from women).

Freud strongly challenges the whole notion of femininity and masculinity as indicative of different psychological characteristics. He argues that psychologically there is no need for such a distinction between men and women—for example, to call men 'active' and women 'passive' has no real basis other than social convention. Indeed he seriously questions whether it is possible to label a woman as being passive at all, when she is so clearly 'active in every sense towards her child'.[6] The description is only true inasmuch as the male sex-cell is active and mobile and seeks out the passive female sex-cell. But in every other respect (Freud appears to argue) these terms are inaccurately imposed by society. The further you go from the sexual sphere the more inaccurate what he calls this 'error of superimposition' (or as we might call it, stereotyping) becomes. 'Women can display great activity in various directions, men are not able to live in company with their own kind unless they develop a large amount of passive adaptability.'[7] We see here how Freud begins to acknowledge, albeit only faintly, that society influences gender differentiation: 'We must beware in this of underestimating the influence of social customs, which similarly force women into passive situations.'[8] This is a point to which I want to return. Yet already there is a hint that he does make some kind of differentiation between women and men: men are less able to live uninhibitedly with others of their own gender than women are with theirs.

On the one hand, therefore, women and men need not be perceived as different: both have the capacity to be active and passive, caring and assertive, logical and intuitive, emotionally tough and emotionally sensitive. Anatomy need not be destiny. Yet Freud simultaneously draws attention to differences, particularly to distinctions in attitude and behaviour. One area already alluded to is that men are less able to live comfortably together without considerable adaptation: a fascinating insight which he does not develop at that point but which perhaps is reflected in the way men tend to 'organize' themselves with rules, hierarchies and tight structures that often leave little room for spontaneity and creativity. This is a subject Freud treats in his book of group psychology.[9]

A second major difference which Freud refers to in these essays on gender is women's and men's attitude to the penis. In his earlier writing the penis is a problem for women: he almost (though not

151

quite) reverses this in his later work when he acknowledges that the penis is more a problem for men. Men disparage women because they regard women as being castrated.[10] Indeed Freud himself appears to be just as disparaging when he uses phrases like 'the inferiority of the clitoris'.[11] But in some respects he is not far from recognizing that just as castration anxiety is a man's problem, so penis envy is too. For the majority of women these are not such important issues, except inasmuch as the penis is a metaphor for male power in society.

What Freud might point to here is the possible differences between women and men in their attitudes to their bodies. On the whole, when women are allowed to speak for themselves, and are not manipulated into becoming sexual objects for men, they are much more comfortable physically with themselves, with others of the same gender and with children, than are men.

A third aspect in which Freud notices a difference between women and men is in moral attitudes. He suggests that women never fully enter the rivalrous struggle for the love of one parent (the Oedipus Complex) with the same intensity as men, and that this explains how they are in some way 'incomplete' in their moral development: 'They show less sense of justice than men . . . they are less ready to submit to the great exigencies of life . . . they are more often influenced in their judgements by feelings of affection or hostility.'[12] Freud's phraseology (at least in translation) is exceedingly unfortunate at times, although to be fair to him, he is here quoting popular opinion about a woman's character-traits. He does so to support his own theory that a girl does not pass through the Oedipus Complex in the same way as a boy, and as a result has a less intense internalization of parental rules—which leads to the formation of what Freud called the 'super-ego', somewhat like the idea of 'conscience'. In fact a less intense super-ego or conscience may be no bad thing, particularly when a sentence or two before these words, he spells out how women's ethical norms are different from men's (not, we note, worse than men's): 'Their super-ego is never so inexorable, so impersonal, so independent of its emotional origins as we require it to be in men.'[13]

Freud only catches a glimpse here of how women may make moral decisions in an important and distinct way. He had little evidence other than a theoretical formulation which is questionable.

Yet unknowingly he anticipates subsequent research, particularly that by Carol Gilligan[14] over fifty years later. She finds clear differences between the way men and women make moral decisions: women stress relationships, men stress rights; women show more understanding of reasons for behaviour than men, even if the behaviour is morally unjustifiable; and women look more at the context and historical reasons that produce moral choices. Gilligan argues that men and women have different conceptions of morality, men focusing on issues of justice, fairness, rules and rights, whereas women emphasize people's wants, needs, interests and aspirations.

This distinction between the way in which women and men approach moral issues may be related to a further distinction between men and women, which has been explicitly stated by feminist therapists, although it is implicit in Freud's observation about men's relationships. In common with many other feminist critics, Chodorow[15] questions the argument put forward by Freud that 'anatomy is destiny'. But she believes that 'Freud's accounts of the psychological destructiveness of bourgeois marriage, gender differentiation and child-rearing practices remain unsurpassed'.[16] She also writes that 'psychoanalytic theory remains the most coherent, convincing theory of personality development for an understanding of fundamental aspects of the psychology of women in our society, in spite of its biases'.[17]

It is superfluous to my argument to extend further Chodorow's own analysis of gender differences, except in two respects. The first is a crucial (and much quoted) assertion that a woman's psyche *is* different: 'The basic feminine sense of self is connected to the world, the basic masculine sense of self is separate.'[18] The second is a necessary balance to the bias towards individual psychopathology which tends to bedevil psychotherapy and also to some extent the moral theology: Chodorow like many other feminist therapists, emphasizes not just the family dynamics which contribute towards gender differences, but also that society 'socializes particular personalities and preferences in girls and boys'.[19]

I have already noted above that Freud catches a glimpse of later work on gender when he hints at the significance of 'social customs' or what we might call socialization. This is in line with his mainstream work where one of his most important theses is that in the conflict between the expectations and norms of society and individual will and desire we find a major cause of neurosis. (No wonder then that women are the main users of mental health services.) Freud's view of this conflict, unlike that of the more radical therapists who have followed him, is that it, and therefore to some extent neurosis (or at least common unhappiness) is inevitable. Feminist therapists, as well as feminist sociologists, have challenged this pessimism, although their suggestions for changing the dynamic relationship between society, family, and gender roles vary greatly. What is clear is that countering sexism cannot take place simply through changing individual attitudes; sexism is also endemic in society, perhaps in the very anatomy of the body politic.

Freud's dilemma (one which was surely a personal one as much as it was a cultural and intellectual one) is how to describe the relationship between the psychology of women and the psychology of men. It is a dilemma which I believe to be a central one for men and women attempting to counter sexism. Freud veers away from the importance of anatomical difference and asserts the essential common identity of men and women in their emotional life. Yet he also recognizes, if only in passing, some equally essential differences between men and women, which may be partly due to the way in which parents relate differently with girls and boys, and partly due to cultural expectations. Men and women are the same, and yet they are different. Freud's anxiety about the feminist analysts of his own generation was that they seemed to put such stress on equality between the sexes as to make differences unimportant.[20] Perhaps he confuses equality within structures with sameness in individual temperament, but I suspect that in this contradiction we see a dilemma and a tension. More positively we can describe this creative tension as an example of what Jung called 'the conjunction of opposites'. It cannot be ignored by those women and men who are trying to correct not just societal inequalities but also the psychological imbalance and splits of the past.

Some Christians are drawn to Jung more than Freud because of his inclusion of the spiritual dimension. His views on gender may seem equally attractive since he apparently arrived at a more balanced view of gender relationships in his theory of the latent or unconscious *anima* (or the feminine) in men, which needs to become more conscious to counter-balance the more obvious aspects of maleness; and the similar (though opposite) unconscious *animus* (or the masculine) in women, likewise necessary to counter-balance their more obviously 'feminine' side. But such neatness, or, to put it another way, such desire for psychological equality certainly makes the following criticism deserving of consideration: 'It does not follow that because men have an Oedipus complex that women have an Electra complex, that because women have an animus that men have an anima'.[21] The Electra Complex was Jung's attempt to find the same (but opposite) complex for girls in relation to their fathers as the Oedipus Complex was for boys in relation to their mothers.

However, this desire for complementarity in Jungian theory carries the risk of carrying a psychological connotation equivalent to Freud's complimenting his women colleagues on being like men when they challenged his theories of child development. Such thinking easily becomes a variant form of patriarchy and patronization. It is male therapists telling women that they are not of course inferior, that they are the equal with men, even that they are 'the same but different'. This looks perilously like male largesse, offering women a place in the complementarity of opposites, making them as necessary to men psychologically as their sexuality is for the fulfilment of male sexuality—men need women to complement themselves. Erikson very obviously gets caught on the horns of a similar dilemma in his essay on women and the inner space, where he holds out the promise of equality; but in recognizing the importance of women he seems to assign to them the inner world of exploration, and to men the outer world of space. Even his references to the necessary presence of women in government or in science employ the term 'representative'.[22] We might wonder if there is not a fear in men that as women find even greater confidence in themselves, they may be tempted to desert men, and to show them that they do not need them psychologically as much as men need women. What men need to be careful of is the wish to appropriate the new ground claimed by women, as much as they have appropriated women sexually, domestically and societally to date.

This psychological appropriation of women as a variant on sexism is a feature in the writing of some leading male psychoanalysts, seen when they try to respond to the criticisms made by their female colleagues. There is the possibility of a similar unconscious sexism in leading men in the Churches, as they change to accommodate the growing confidence of women in their various forms of ministry. The very unconscious nature of such sexism means that it is not shown, of course, by those who are blatanily sexist, but rather by those who think themselves enlightened, or by those men who have taken the feminist perspective seriously. It is all the more dangerous for that.

This unconscious sexism takes at least two opposite forms. The first is that of men accepting women into their world, and yet at the same time demonstrating their need to hang on to power. It is perhaps inevitable that because men predominate in many 'worlds' that they have to be the ones who 'let women in', but in so doing they continue to maintain male supremacy. Women are admitted to full membership by men, and not as a result of their own action (only as a result of their pressure). What is worse is that women are then often expected to be grateful to enlightened men, and to show their gratitude by adopting and adapting to male rules developed by male members of an old all-male club. So sexism continues, but now less easy to confront, because it often needs to be fought in those who imagine themselves allies of the women's cause.

The dilemma which many feminists face (including some women who have opposed the ordination of women, but not from the usual position) is this: do you join them, and risk losing your identity as a woman? Or do you adopt a separatist stance, on the ground that the male world is not that desirable a one to join? In any case, if you join, the odds are stacked against changing anything. Furthermore, this is made more difficult for many women because, as Chodorow suggests, while 'most women do develop a sense of separate self . . . separation and individuation remain particularly female developmental issues'.[23] Sexism may take the form of incorporating women, thereby making it more difficult for them to be themselves, and harder for them to develop their own unique way of being. What we need to look to, therefore, is not only the empowering of women in order that they may, if they choose, achieve all that men can in terms of status and position and power in society. Women also have to be empowered to refuse what men want to offer them. They may not like either what they are offered or indeed that it is offered at all.

This first type of unconscious sexism is largely sexism by men against women. The second variation is unconscious sexism against men as well. It is apparent in the desire by those who call themselves 'New Men' to blur gender differences, and to identify with women rather than with men. At first they appear to adopt a totally correct position. They do not like the way the conventional man in our society is brought up to be.

There is a lot of truth, of course, in what these New Men say. Men often lack the ability to feel, or at least to own their feelings to others. They often lack the ability to empathize as sensitively as women can with the dilemmas and pains which others experience. Men prefer to act rather than be; to analyse rather than sympathize; to explain, rationalize and moralize rather than protest. They lack the ability to work co-operatively without imposing such rules and order upon the corporate, that they threaten to kill, and almost always to some extent strangle the life of the body. In addition, and this applies to the intimate as well as the corporate, they frequently lack the ability to share themselves at any depth with other men — where they choose a confidante it is frequently a woman.

Such analysis and criticism has much of value in it, and is one which cannot be ignored. The sexist element comes not so much in the content of the argument, but in the way in which New Man turns upon his own gender. As one comment puts it: 'To be a Real Macho Man, you had to act as if you were God's gift to women: now, to be a Real New Man, you have to own up to being the booby prize. "Christ, we men are all such bastards!" is the boast of all Real New Men. . . . Women must not try to be "like men"; men, however, must be more "like women" (which takes for granted the whole sexist package of biological determinism).'[24]

Similarly feminists often show the same sexism when they talk about 'men', as if they are all the same and there is no difference between them: the issue of sameness and difference applies equally to the way women and men talk in general terms about the opposite gender. There is an important sense in which we need to

Michael Jacobs

be able to say 'Men are . . .' and 'Women are . . .'; but it is equally important to recognize that men and women are individuals too within their own gender groups.

The New Man frequently becomes a New Man through contact with the women's movement, and then turns to women's groups, often apparently seeking help to change. I do not mean to question the necessity for men to make a radical re-appraisal of what it is to be a man, particularly of what men lack, both within themselves and within their relationships, in interpersonal as well as in societal terms. But not unnaturally, given a long history of male entrenchment, some women are suspicious of New Men, wondering what unconscious motives these men have for their change of heart. And indeed they are right to reverse the famous question Freud put of women, and ask 'What does *man* want?'[25] In this they have the support of the realism of the Freudian (as indeed the Pauline) analysis of the human condition, with its recognition of the persistent strength of the unconscious feelings and motives. This reinforces the suspicion of where has the 'Old Man' got to, of whether the 'New Man' is still the old Adam beneath, and whether men are still wolves, who imagine that they can become lambs overnight.

The 'Old Man' may still be there under the guise of joining the women's movement: men still cannot leave women alone to their own area of societal concern. It may be all right leaving women to the kitchen and the nursery, but the women's movement is challenging male territory: and if you can't beat them, join them. So the New Man may even start to take over women's claims, and try to become the Prince who fights women's battles for them— 'Leave this to me, darling'. Unconsciously—and because it is unconsciously, even more powerfully—the New Man continues patriarchy and domination under the guise of support. There is furthermore another way in which the old appears under the guise of the new: because not only did the 'Old Man' want women to cook his meals, bear and bring up his children, mend his clothes, and be good in bed; now the New Man wants his women not only to help him change, but to nurture, provide and protect him through the process.

Such criticism may seem harsh, although it is one which is

being increasingly voiced by women as they watch more and more men adopt, or apparently adopt, a feminist position. There is in the unconscious sexism of the New Man a danger for women, of being trapped into the submissive caring role. There is the danger for men that they will put on the feminist position like a new set of clothes, in place of expecting women to fit into the patterns which men have created. Yet these men may seek to fit themselves into what they assume women want, but without actually discovering themselves first. They have in the past been able to distance from themselves by virtue of their emphasis on status, hierarchies, rules, order and power. There is a present danger, especially for the so-called 'New Men' who make a move away from traditionally male ways of conducting society and themselves, that they will then be distanced from themselves by trying to become like women. Either way they may fail to find out who they really are, and fail to see how they unconsciously behave towards each other and towards women.

There is something about masculinity and about being a man which consists in more than learning to accept the anima (in Jungian terms); and in more than encouraging the development of that side of themselves which women appear more 'naturally' to possess—whether it is nurture or nature that engenders it. Although there is a danger in talking about the 'feminine', or even in talking about discovering the 'masculine', the evidence frequently is that women, having found something for themselves, do not then want men to come and take that over too. They would prefer men to discover for themselves what is important to them as men, and not to copy women, any more than men should demand that women copy them.

So the distinctions may actually be important. It may be necessary to acknowledge more strongly than we have yet done that there is indeed a sense in which anatomy, if not exactly destiny, is about difference. Not only in child-bearing but also through practices of child-rearing there do appear to be certain differences between women and men. These may have been culturally reinforced to the mutual disadvantage of both, but nonetheless there is a distinctiveness which is equally capable in the future of mutual benefit. How this may come about we do not yet know. But women's groups, and men's groups, and the equal dialogue between the two will be one important way in which sexism and gender issues are faced up to within the Church.

Notes

1. The Penguin Freud Library (PFL) Volume 7 (*On Sexuality*) collects together a number of Freud's writings which are relevant to gender as much as to sexuality. The phrase 'Anatomy is Destiny' appears in *The Tendency to Debasement in Love* (PFL: 7, 1912), p. 259 and *The Dissolution of the Oedipus Complex* (PFL: 7, 1924), p. 320.
2. *Introductory Lectures on Psychoanalysis*, PFL: Vol. 1.
3. *New Introductory Lectures on Psychoanalysis*, PFL: Vol. 2.
4. ibid., p. 150.
5. ibid., p. 151.
6. ibid., p. 148.
7. ibid., p. 148.
8. ibid., p. 149.
9. *Group Psychology and the Analysis of the Ego*. PFL: Vol. 12.
10. PFL: Vol. 7, p. 376.
11. ibid., p. 339.
12. ibid., p. 342.
13. ibid., p. 342.
14. Gilligan, C., *In a Different Voice*. Mass., Harvard University Press, 1982.
15. Chodorow, N., *The Reproduction of Mothering*. London, Yale University Press, 1978.
16. Chodorow (1978), p. 40.
17. ibid., p. 142.
18. ibid., p. 169.
19. ibid., p. 25.
20. PFL: Vol. 7, p. 377.
21. Downing, C., 'Gender Anxiety', in *Journal of Pastoral Care* (USA), XLIII: 2, p. 154.
22. Erikson, E., 'Womanhood and the Inner Space', in *Identity: Youth and Crisis*. London, Faber and Faber, 1968.
23. Chodorow (1978), p. 110.
24. 'Self-hate' by Cosmo Landesman. *The Guardian*, 20 June 1990.
25. Freud told Marie Bonaparte that he had been doing research into 'the feminine soul' for thirty years and had little to show for it. 'What does woman want?', he asked. See Gay, P., *Freud: a Life for Our Time* (London, Macmillan, 1989), p. 501.

RICHARD HOLLOWAY

Postscript:
Feminism and the General Synod

I was a student in New York city in the 1960s and I remember distinctly my discomfort with the emergence of Black Power and Black Theology. Like every humane person, I was a supporter of the Civil Rights Movement in its early, polite and respectful phase, but I became increasingly unhappy as Black Americans became more assertive and angry. It was a Dominican priest who helped me through the predicament. A Frenchman, he was preparing himself for ministry in South America, where he has been for the last twenty-five years, working in total identification with the poor. Ile was a disciple of Paolo Friere and he told me about his revolutionary educational method called 'conscientization'. He reminded me that it was very difficult for any dominant group to get into the consciousness of oppressed or dominated people. Two things had to happen. The oppressed had to learn how to assert themselves, how to move from a slave to a free mentality; and the oppressing group had to let its consciousness be altered so that it could understand the nature of its own oppressive activity. Black Power and Black Theology were necessary aspects of the change in consciousness that had to occur if the African American community was to take its place as equal in the eyes of the law and in the eyes of God. A large part of that process of change involved language about black people, because language informs and articulates unconscious attitudes. Language is sacramental. It effects what it signifies. Certainly, few wise and fair-minded people today would doubt the importance of listening to black people when they try to explain to the white community why its language and the unconscious attitudes it betrays are painful and offensive to them. In struggling for a society purged of racism, a society that foreshadows, even if it does not yet fully reflect, the kingdom of God, we have to allow our consciousness to be challenged and changed. We have to repent of the old, sinful attitudes and seek a more righteous society. Listening to the cry of the oppressed and

161

really understanding the nature of their pain is an important part of the change of consciousness that Christians call repentance. What the good Dominican priest taught me was confirmed vividly when I heard James Baldwin speak at a Civil Rights rally in Battery Park, on the tip of Manhattan. His angry eloquence convinced me that Black Americans had to move away from the conservative and respectful image exemplified by Dr Martin Luther King and challenge the nature of American society to its very roots.

I was back in the USA in the early 1980s. The agenda of protest had changed, but again I was reluctant to listen. The focus of the debate had already shifted from the ordination of women to religious language. I was, and still am, a lover of traditional liturgical language and I could not understand why it offended these mysteriously angry women who confronted me. My attitude gradually changed as I listened to women and began to understand their pain, and finally to identify with it. If a large number of people tell me that they feel offended by my attitudes and language, I have to listen to them, if only because I come from a religious tradition that values prophecy. To be on the receiving end of prophetic anger is never comfortable, which is why prophets in scripture usually end up being stoned. It is also worth remembering that biblical prophecy usually focuses its anger on the liturgy. It denounces it as offensive to God, because it is oppressive and anodyne at the same time, lulling the worshippers into a kind of cultic narcosis that ignores the pain of the excluded.

What to me is the multitude of your sacrifices? says the Lord;
I have had enough of burnt offerings of rams and the fat of fed beasts;
I do not delight in the blood of bulls, or of lambs, or of he-goats.

When you come to appear before me, who requires of you this trampling of my courts?
Bring no more vain offerings; incense is an abomination to me.
New moon and sabbath and the calling of assemblies —
I cannot endure iniquity and solemn assembly.
Your new moons and your appointed feasts my souls hates;

they have become a burden to me, I am weary of bearing them.
When you spread forth your hands, I will hide my eyes from
   you;
even though you make many prayers, I will not listen;
your hands are full of blood.
Wash yourselves; make yourselves clean;
remove the evil of your doings from before my eyes;
cease to do evil, learn to do good;
seek justice, correct oppression;
defend the fatherless, plead for the widow.

Isaiah 1:11-18

This great diatribe against the liturgical system has become part
of *our* service, but it must have been as offensive to the priests of
Israel as feminist theology is to many Christian priests today.

Part of the paradoxical dynamism of biblical religion is that
the God whom scripture reveals will not allow us to make idols
of anything, not excluding scripture. God's righteousness is
paramount and it calls us to question every human concentration
of power that oppresses, even if it is found at the most sacred
centre of the liturgy. This is why people like John Broadhurst,
who are genuinely trying to understand the feminist perspective,
must put down their weapons of defence and start listening
deeply to the pain of women in the Church. In his paper on
feminist theology for the General Synod of July 1991, Broadhurst
shows that he has listened to and understood some of that pain
and anger. He understands, and to some extent sympathises
with, feminine anger against Human Patriarchy, but he cannot
entertain the possibility that it has influenced theology or is
found in scripture itself. But is it likely that what he calls the
'objective revelation' of God in scripture will have been
mysteriously protected in its expression from the historical
conditioning that characterises the texts as we have them? We
know we have this treasure in earthen vessels. Simply to claim
that the vessels are as indestructible as fine gold does not make
them so. But the important thing is to have the discussion or the
debate in the first place. This is why Broadhurst's call for an
investigation is to be welcomed, but it will only work if there are
no reserved areas. Those who are happy with religious language

as we presently use it must try to hear what is being said by those who are offended by it, without jumping to the conclusion that it is God who is under attack. God does not really need our protection; and language about God is not, anyway, the same thing *as* God, though the current brands of semantic idolatry at both extremes of the feminist debate seem to suggest that it is. What is needed is an injection of apophatic theology into the debate, the recognition that all our language about God is oblique, provisional and, at its best, only analogical. The Old Testament writers knew this well, which was why they rarely named God directly and preferred to speak periphrastically.

And John Broadhurst must not poison the wells by lumping all feminists together. Daphne Hampson and Mary Daly no longer claim to be Christians, but Monica Furlong, with whom he identifies them, is hanging in there against all the odds.

But why this high anxiety? Christian theology has been in constant flux since Jesus told us he came to bring not the peace of the graveyard but the sword of the spirit.

The only serious enemy of God is idolatry. Idolatry gives absolute value to relative things, it is the fraudulent claim that a temporal object is the specific location of the divine. It is a way of controlling the divine by fixing it to one place. Idolatry is a paranoid version of sacramentalism. In a sacrament God comes to us *through* an object; in idolatry God is *in* an object, so the *object* is viewed as divine. The tendency to idolatry, to assert that God is *in* a thing, is almost inescapable and has to be constantly resisted. And it can operate in reverse. Many defenders of traditional theological language, such as John Broadhurst, fall into the trap of identifying God with language about God; but some of the people he opposes fall into the opposite trap of wanting, not his version of linguistic idolatry, a language that contains God, but their own version, their own idol. This is why there is so little humour in the debate: idolatrists are rarely able to laugh at their own obsessions. But the debate ought not to be over rival idolatries, but over the nature of language in its sacramental role as a conveyer of the divine mystery. That is a debate worth having. It is in no one's interest to conduct the matter like a dispute between rival sects of the Priests of Baal. Isaiah should have the first word: 'Come now, let us *reason* together, says the Lord' (Isa. 1.18).